THE CREATIVE ADVANCE

THE
CREATIVE ADVANCE

*An Introduction to Process Philosophy as
a Context for Christian Faith*

by Eugene H. Peters

With a comment by Charles Hartshorne

B

THE BETHANY PRESS · ST. LOUIS, MISSOURI
1966

Distributed by Thomas C. Lothian, Melbourne,
Australia, and Auckland, New Zealand and by
The G. R. Welch Company, Toronto, Canada

An Introductory Statement

"THE NEW THEOLOGY," a phrase appearing with some frequency in the decade of the 1960's, has not as yet acquired a clearly defined meaning. Its very currency, however, signifies the emergence of certain discernible trends in theological reflection. Two things can be said about it with reasonable confidence.

The first is that around us on every hand are signs that history has come to one of those rare and momentous turning-of-the-tides in human existence. These signs appear in the new mathematics and the revolutionary physics which have given us nuclear power, electronic "think-and-do" machines, instant world-wide communication, and space travel; in abstract painting, atonal music, and shocking and exciting new forms of drama and poetry; in depth psychology, open-heart surgery, and the "population explosion"; in the ecumenical movement within Protestantism and the Vatican Council of the Roman Catholic Church.

Not since the sixteenth and seventeenth centuries have so many great minds engaged themselves in giving us new conceptual forms in which to articulate new forms of life and thought. Then theologians like Luther and Erasmus, Pascal and Calvin; scientists such as Galileo, Johannes Kepler, and Isaac Newton; philosophers like René Descartes, Francis Bacon, and Baruch Spinoza; dramatists including William Shakespeare and Miguel de Cervantes; the painters El Greco, Rubens, and Rembrandt; statesmen like Cardinal Richelieu and Oliver Cromwell; political scientists such as Hugo Grotius, and many

5

others shaped the ideas and events that rewrote the terms of human existence. The modern age was born.

Now we have apparently come to the end of the "modern" epoch. Mankind travails in a new birth. Every high school student knows the names of Albert Einstein, Niels Bohr, Sigmund Freud, Pablo Picasso, Arnold Schoenberg, and James Joyce. These and others are heralds of a new epoch. The twentieth century promises to be one of the great watersheds of history.

What will this century mean in terms of religious reflection and theological reconstruction? It is as yet too early to answer that question. But all who read and think today are aware that something of tremendous importance is happening in biblical studies, social ethics, systematic theology, and philosophy. One need not lose himself in the libraries of the universities and theological seminaries to be familiar with the names of Karl Barth, Paul Tillich, Reinhold Niebuhr, Emil Brunner, Alfred North Whitehead, Martin Buber, Rudolf Bultmann, Jacques Maritain, and Dietrich Bonhoeffer. One meets them in the secular journals and in parlor conversations. Such terms as existentialism, alienation, paradox, encounter, creativity, the courage to be, and religionless Christianity are current literary coinage.

But whatever shape "the new theology" may take, it will owe an incalculable debt to these theologians of the middle third of this century who have already altered irreversibly the directions of theological thought and the terms of theological debate.

This book is one of several to appear with the Bethany Press imprint in the next few years under the general title, "Library of Contemporary Theology." This series of small books is intended to help open doors into this new world of ideas for those nonprofessional theologians of many callings who have neither time nor opportunity to wrestle long and hard with the massive thought of the great thinkers of our time, those whose ideas have already entered into the stream of our religious understanding, and will influence it for generations to come. It is hoped also that these books may serve as introductions to these thinkers and their thought for university and theological students whose special tasks require them to seek some guiding clues to what are often highly technical and dense systems. In any case, the intention is to lead those interested into reading with comprehension the works of these theological leaders who are at the cutting edge of religious conceptualization in our time and whose works constitute new starting points for our understanding of the situation of man in the world before God.

Walter W. Sikes
GENERAL EDITOR

Preface

THIS BOOK IS INTENDED as an introduction to "process philosophy," one of the most adequate interpretations of reality ever devised. Although the book is concerned with the whole of process philosophy, it is especially concerned with those features which have a theological bearing. An entire chapter (Chapter V) is devoted to the doctrine of God in the thought of Alfred North Whitehead, the constructive genius of process philosophy. In addition, major attention (Chapters VI and VII) is given to the development of the theological side of process thought in Charles Hartshorne's work. There can, however, be little doubt that process philosophy, taken in its essence, is a "spiritual" philosophy and is in alignment with the attitude and outlook of men of religion.

To speak of *process* philosophy is to suggest the idea that reality is at base dynamic and changing. Indeed, for process philosophy God himself is not static. Of course, a changing whole may contain (may even require) fixed parts. Process philosophers have no interest in stripping the world of all permanence. Their intent is rather to conceive the world with process as the *inclusive* category. The ultimate units of reality are seen to be "drops of experience" emerging as actualities by virtue of their relatedness to past actualities. Ceaseless, creative advance from the settled past to the (relatively) novel present is the most fundamental character of reality. Anything whatsoever must be interpreted as a fact or factor within the creative advance.

Obviously, we are dealing with a world view, a metaphysical system, not a doctrine about certain aspects or special features

9

of the world. Chapter I furnishes a general account of the nature and task of a metaphysical system. Chapter II is concerned with the world view generated by modern science in the seventeenth century, a world view that has persisted doggedly and exerts influence even today. Based upon physics and common sense, it sees the world in which we live as a mechanism, having neither feeling nor purpose, but moving with mathematical regularity. The world "outside" is then utterly discontinuous with the world "inside," that is, with experience and thought. Hence, we have a physical-psychical dualism on our hands. In Chapter III Whitehead's response to this dualism is examined. His system is presented in fuller and more technical form in Chapter IV.

The book is largely expository. Even if the reader is inclined to argue the case with the process philosophers, he will not deny the importance of attending to what they actually say. However, not all is exposition. Chapter VIII gathers up various process themes of importance for Christian thought (without claiming to be exhaustive), and Chapter IX, the last chapter in the book, offers some criticism of process philosophy.

No book can be all things to all men. But in writing the book, the author had two groups especially in mind. First, he was thinking of those to whom it is chiefly addressed: readers who, while interested in philosophy and theology, are professionals in neither field. In this group are ministers, inquiring laymen, students, and the like. Second, he was thinking of competent process scholars, who will read this book with an eye to its accuracy, clarity, comprehensiveness, and so forth. These two groups have somewhat different concerns and criteria. If the book does not please both, perhaps it will displease neither.

A generous grant from Hiram College in the summer of 1963 freed me for months of full-time work on the book. I am deeply grateful to the College for providing me this rare opportunity. I wish also to express my gratitude for assistance and encouragement received from a number of able persons. Professor Bernard M. Loomer of the Berkeley Baptist Divinity School and the

Graduate Theological Union read early drafts of several chapters. I am indebted to him for his helpful comments as well as for his interest. I have a double debt to Professor Charles Hartshorne of the University of Texas, who read the manuscript and (at a number of points) suggested improvements, and then wrote the comment which is included at the end of this volume. My thanks are also due Mrs. Hartshorne, who carefully read the manuscript and not only edited out a number of errors in usage, but helped with various theoretical and interpretive points as well. I was fortunate in having still another reader, Hunter Beckelhymer of Brite Divinity School, Texas Christian University, who read almost the entire manuscript and gave me the benefit of a minister's appraisal of it. I am grateful to him for a number of suggestions as well as for the questions he raised here and there. My editor, Professor Walter Sikes, has aided me with the manuscript from start to finish. His help with matters of organization, style, and wording, and also with the substance of the book, has enabled me to present to the reader a much finer product than would otherwise have been possible. I am grateful to Mrs. Velma Thrasher, faculty secretary at Hiram College, for her part in typing the manuscript. My wife, Damaris, has helped at various stages with the typing. Also, she has read the entire manuscript and discussed it with me, and in many other ways she has helped and supported me in this effort.

Contents

CHAPTER I

The Philosophical Hedgehog

> . . . *the history of philosophy in the twentieth century is a history of hedgehogs and foxes, a history of philosophers who strive to know one big thing and those who are content to know many little things, or indeed one little thing.*
>
> Morton White[1]

M. SEARLE BATES of Union Theological Seminary, New York, tells of an incident which occurred in a meeting of the zoology department of a great university. During the meeting the question arose as to what courses would be offered the following year. One by one the professors reported their intended offerings. The number of highly specialized courses soon grew sizable as each professor listed his favorite facets of zoology. Finally, one of the professors, a man of years and distinction, asked almost tearfully: "Can't we have just one course dealing with *animals*?"

There was wisdom in his remark—not only for zoologists but for all of us. Accustomed as we are to thinking in compartments, we forget that the world is somehow one world. Strangely, the world, in all its variety and complexity, hangs together.

---

[1]From *The Age of Analysis* (Boston: Houghton Mifflin Company, 1955), p. 18. Used by permission.

By division of labor, we concern ourselves with this, that, or the other feature of it, but the task of considering the "whole animal" is an inescapable responsibility.

Many try to keep religion isolated from the remainder of life and thought. Each of us knows someone or other (perhaps ourselves!) who tries to keep religion hermetically sealed off from science or philosophy. If religion is more than a Sunday morning affair, if, indeed, it involves the whole man, should it not be brought into contact with every deed, desire, attitude, or idea a man has? The theologian, whose task is to formulate the meaning of the faith, cannot permit himself to become a religious introvert. He must face the question as to how things fit together to form one world—a world in which men can meaningfully worship and serve God.

Through the ages various philosophers have sought to present a vision of the whole of things, and Christian theologians have worked within the context of such philosophical visions. For example, Augustine owes much to the philosophy of Plato, Aquinas much to that of Aristotle. Today a new vision of reality has been wrought by the labor of philosophers. The world is seen as dynamic, moving, changing—so that process becomes the fundamental category of interpretation. Many minds have contributed, directly or indirectly, to the development of this new philosophical outlook. The American philosopher William James and the French philosopher Henri Bergson were among its forerunners. The English philosopher Samuel Alexander is one of its contemporary representatives. But the Einstein of process philosophy is Alfred North Whitehead, who died in 1947 after a long and brilliant career in Great Britain and the United States. Charles Hartshorne, a distinguished American process philosopher and interpreter of Whitehead, enjoys a growing influence among theologians.

Process philosophy affords the Christian theologian a powerful instrument by which to interpret the world, an instrument which theologians in this country (many of them young men) are using with great effectiveness. Indeed, in recent decades a loose-knit school of process theology has emerged in the United States. With this school we may associate the names of Bernard Meland of the University of Chicago; Bernard Loomer of the Berkeley Baptist Divinity School and the Graduate Theological Union; Daniel Williams of Union Theological Seminary, New York; Schubert Ogden of Southern Methodist University; and John Cobb of the Claremont School of Theology. The work of these and other process theologians furnishes one solid point of contact between contemporary theology and contemporary British-American philosophy. More generally, it represents a new meeting of theology with culture. Our aim in the pages ahead is to explore process philosophy as a framework for theological thought, paying special attention to some of the chief doctrines of Whitehead and Hartshorne.

The process philosopher undertakes to see life steadily and see it whole (to paraphrase Matthew Arnold). He seeks a synoptic vision, a global view of things. In a word he is, in the philosopher's vocabulary, a metaphysician. Some theologians fear any sort of alliance with metaphysics; they argue that during the last century theology was so in league with philosophy that it lost rootage in its own distinctive sources and tended to wither away. Many philosophers in our day are also suspicious of metaphysics, and some of them reject it outright. But metaphysics is as old (and as young) as man, and it meets man's undeniable need to comprehend the world's oneness. Not only does process metaphysics correct certain excesses in classical philosophy, not only does it take into account modern advances in science and the humanities, but, in addition, it provides an interpretation of reality which is congenial to the biblical-Christian concept of God and the world. Indeed, process metaphysics promises to be a most fruitful context for theological endeavor—one which no theologian can afford to ignore.

What, more precisely, is metaphysics? We are not concerned so much with the dictionary definition of the term as with the motive or intent underlying the metaphysical enterprise. This is not to say that the dictionary definition is of no importance.

17

In a day when technical terms from physics, medicine, etc., often become household words, there is no reason why some of the basic terms of philosophy, terms such as "metaphysics," should not have greater currency. But to say as does my small dictionary that metaphysics is "that branch of philosophy which treats of first principles, including the sciences of being *(ontology)* and of the origin and structure of the universe *(cosmology)*"[2] may tend to bewilder rather than illumine the reader.

It would be incorrect to claim that scientists describe *how* things occur while metaphysicians explain (or try to explain) *why* they occur. A scientist, it is true, makes and reports observations, but this is by no means the whole story, for he is interested in the pattern which events exhibit. If he can discover such a pattern, he will then have a key by which to unify and order things which otherwise appear quite unrelated. The fall of an apple might seem to have little to do with the orbiting of the planets, but Newton's gravitational law expresses the principle exhibited by both. Mere description of fact occasions all kinds of questions, even to a scientifically untrained mind. Any parent can testify to that. Only a few days ago a six-year-old boy, who is currently interested in the art of sowing and growing, asked why seeds when planted in the earth come up and seem never to make the mistake of going down. The fact that seeds do come up is obvious enough, but it fails to satisfy even a child's craving to understand. Facts tease the mind to uncover their secrets, and the mind leaps ahead, guessing at their interpretation. Scientists often hit upon their most fruitful insights when perplexed by plain facts. It seems misleading, therefore, to say that scientists merely describe how things happen.

On the other hand, the claim that metaphysicians seek not to describe how but to explain why things occur may possibly suggest that metaphysicians are concerned with some fanciful realm beyond space and time. Indeed, does not the very word

---

[2]*The American College Dictionary*, ed. Clarence L. Barnhart (New York: Random House, 1951), p. 765. I use "metaphysics" and "ontology" as synonyms,

"metaphysics" suggest some such notion? The process metaphysicians with whom this book is concerned would flatly deny that they are discussing a transcendent world. For example, Charles Hartshorne states:

Metaphysics is the study of ideas universally applicable. These ideas define being *qua* being, the widest universe of discourse, or the universe of "all time and all existence." Thus metaphysical does not mean behind or above the physical (or the observable), but all through the physical (or observable), and all through everything else, if anything else there be.[3]

If metaphysics is the study of ideas universally applicable, it appears that metaphysics and science are not wholly unlike one another. Both seek to interpret the facts of experience. But science is departmentalized according to the variety of subject matters examined (though the demarcation between departments may be rather fuzzy), while metaphysics is the study of ideas applicable all through the physical (or observable), as Hartshorne says. Indeed, if metaphysical ideas are universally applicable, they embrace even the regions of thought and experience which lie beyond the legitimate boundaries of science— if (as Hartshorne says) such there be.

The metaphysician is fired by the desire to map the ultimate dimensions of the universe. He is interested not so much in the general features which the universe *happens* to exhibit at this particular period in cosmic history as he is in those structures or principles which any universe whatsoever would have to exhibit. Thus, the metaphysician is concerned with those characteristics which are common to any and all things. Amid the obvious multiplicity and diversity of things, he tries to identify an outline so basic as to cover any possible fact. To see unity within diversity is itself a major function of intelligence, if it is not part of the very meaning of the term. If a person were to answer the question, "How is a basketball like a grapefruit?" by declaring that they are not alike, since a basketball is used

---

[3]Charles Hartshorne, "Metaphysics for Positivists," *Philosophy of Science,* II (July, 1935), 288. Used by permission of the Williams & Wilkins Co.

for play but a grapefruit is eaten, we would be inclined to regard such a person as retarded. Intelligence demands to be apprised of the order and connection of things, to see the forest and not just the trees. This does not deny the importance of seeing the trees, that is, of attending to the facts in all their variety and richness. But the mind needs a telescope as well as a microscope; and while many of his philosophical colleagues busy themselves with detailed analysis, the metaphysician sets his sights on achieving the global, synthetic view.

The metaphysician holds that all things ultimately hang together in a rational way; that at base things are not just arbitrarily related—like strangers who chance to sit beside one another on a bus; in short, that the world has an intelligible constitution. But the metaphysician is not thereby obliged to deny the reality of chance, spontaneity, freedom, and flux. It was the nineteenth-century German philosopher Hegel who by his example fastened upon modern thought the erroneous notion that in the metaphysician's hands the whole world shrivels into a rational system. If such alchemy were the metaphysician's aim, revolt against metaphysics would be entirely justified. What he seeks is the world's context, not its content.

The metaphysician assumes an affinity between mind and the world structure. Thus, metaphysics is grounded on a rationalistic trust. To say, however, that the nature of things is not opaque to reason is not to claim that any metaphysician has ever fully grasped it (or ever will). It is rather to affirm that in his probings the metaphysician will encounter no impenetrable walls from which he must retreat, baffled and frustrated. Yet, as Alfred North Whitehead points out, lack of imagination and deficiency in language make the approach to first principles exceedingly difficult. Whitehead holds, in fact, that "philosophers can never hope finally to formulate these metaphysical first principles."[4]

---

[4]Alfred North Whitehead, *Process and Reality* (New York: The Macmillan Company, 1929), p. 6.

One wonders how the metaphysician makes any progress at all toward the lofty heights to which he aspires. The special difficulty he confronts is that principles which are exemplified everywhere are terrifically hard to see. One sees most readily the things that are (or at least may be) sometimes absent. If, for example, my next-door neighbor drives by in a brand-new car, I take note of it because I am accustomed to his driving another car. But to try to observe anything that is permanent and omnipresent is a rather different matter. It is a little like trying to look directly into one's own eyes. What is the metaphysician's method of attack? Following certain of the process philosophers here, we may say that the metaphysician begins in some particular area of human thought or experience, seizes the most basic ideas in that area, and then attempts to apply them beyond that area and indeed universally. The crucial question is: what is the scope of any given metaphysical hypothesis? To what extent does it furnish an overall interpretation of things? The metaphysician uses deduction in order to help find an answer to this question. In the past some philosophers have assumed that they could begin with self-evident axioms and from them deduce the content of reality. But as Hartshorne says, "The true role of deduction in metaphysics is not to bring out the content of the initially certain, but to bring out the meaning of tentative descriptions of the metaphysically ultimate in experience so that we shall be better able to judge if they do genuinely describe this ultimate."[5]

Thus, the metaphysician, like the scientist, employs the "working hypothesis." He may take a principle from physics, say the principle of relativity, and try to formulate it in such a way that it can be seen to apply beyond physics. The principle is then a metaphysical hypothesis, put forth as a possible description of the very nature of things. A metaphysical hypothesis need not originate in one of the sciences. Business, religion, art, recreation, or any other area of human life and interest

---

[5]Hartshorne, *Reality as Social Process* (Glencoe, Ill.: The Free Press, 1953), p. 175. Use by permission.

may provide the metaphysician a germ idea. For example, he might take from music the notion that harmony is diversity within unity and explore the possibility of finding application for that notion in the other arts and beyond. In any event, he does not pull his ideas out of a hat; his procedure is to extend ideas which are known to apply throughout a given field. Thus, he is assured that at least some region of thought or experience can be interpreted in terms of those ideas he advances as candidates for the ultimate generalities. Whitehead regards this as a basic requirement in metaphysics. "The true method of discovery is like the flight of an aeroplane," he says. "It starts from the ground of particular observation; it makes a flight in the thin air of imaginative generalization; and it again lands for renewed observation rendered acute by rational interpretation."[6] When the metaphysician takes off from "the ground of particular observation," he must, says Whitehead, be guided in his imaginative flight by logical rigor and by the aim at a coherent structure of thought. Of course, the acid test of a metaphysical scheme is whether it provides a comprehensive interpretation of things—in Whitehead's words, whether it is adequate.

Perhaps this is enough to suggest what metaphysics is about— at least from the point of view of certain process thinkers. No one should miss the importance of the fact that the metaphysician is trying to see life in its wholeness, not just piecemeal. In a day of specialization he is one bird who is really trying for the bird's-eye view. Many of his colleagues in philosophy have largely abandoned this task—despite the fact that philosophers throughout history have taken it as their central business. Thus, within present-day philosophy the metaphysician is a hedgehog among foxes, intent on seeing the shape of the whole rather than fastening only on minute and isolated matters.[7] I am convinced that the philosophical hedgehogs can help bring sanity to our thought and even to our lives. Someone will

---

[6]Whitehead, *op. cit.*, p. 7. Used by permission.
[7]See Morton White (ed.), *The Age of Analysis*, p. 18.

perhaps argue that the universe is mysterious and simply defies comprehension. He may add that God at any rate is beyond human understanding, as Christian theologians have always held. This objection oversimplifies things. To be sure, some metaphysicians have tried to reduce everything to logic. But to "unscrew the inscrutable" is not part of the metaphysician's job description. He is trying to comprehend the world's logical framework, which may indeed enclose unfathomable mysteries. It seems to me that there is nothing contradictory about this; ideas never exhaust the facts which they interpret.

Suppose a young man says to his sweetheart, "I love only you," and she replies, "And what's so special about me?" The young man then has a problem on his hands. He is certain that she is different from all other girls, but just how? He takes a crack at it: "You're pretty and besides you have a wonderful personality." "Marjorie and Jane and dozens of other girls are pretty and have wonderful personalities." "But nobody has a sense of humor like yours, and nobody's as smart." "Couldn't there be another girl with a sense of humor like mine and just as smart? I hope you're not in love with just a type of girl!" Pondering the matter, the young man may conclude, and rightly, that his sweetheart's uniqueness is beyond finding out, no matter how much he knows about her. In much the same way, the world possesses mystery which no knowledge can dissolve. The same is true of the Deity. Relative to this point, Hartshorne comments: "That about God which reason cannot know is not the essence of God, that which he is in general terms, such as all-knowing, or loving; but the particular form that this knowing or loving takes when a given particular creature is its object."[8] Reason can never catch the unique, the concrete, the particular in its net—a net capable of girdling the entire universe without squeezing the life out of it.

Someone may raise a question as to the practical possibility of doing metaphysics. How in this day can anyone span the vari-

---

[8] Hartshorne, *Reality as Social Process*, p. 171. Used by permission.

ous sciences and humanities in an effort to formulate and test a metaphysical hypothesis? Admittedly, the required scope of knowledge is breathtaking, and there are few universal geniuses. But it seems to me that the mind is such a curious and restless seeker that it will forever refuse to be confined within specialized fields, despite the counsel of practical men. Of course, many will prefer the familiarity and security of their own bailiwicks, but always a few adventurers will embark on the "voyage towards the larger generalities."[9] In the United States there are a number of such adventurers in ideas whose achievements encourage one to believe that the metaphysical task, difficult though it is, is not beyond possibility. In the future, the serious problem of covering a multitude of areas may have to be met by some form of teamwork. Already such projects are under way in this country. It is important, however, to keep in mind that the metaphysician is not looking for a needle in a haystack. He is trying to grasp principles which are universal and which are therefore ever present in his own experience. The truth is that "metaphysics can only make us more conscious of what we already know."[10] That is, metaphysics can present us nothing absolutely new, but it can enable us to discern more distinctly those universal principles of which we are always dimly aware. "Only the degree of consciousness counts in philosophical insight," says Hartshorne. "There is no such thing as complete human ignorance or perfect human understanding of any philosophical truth."[11] Conceivably, a metaphysician with extensive knowledge in the sciences and humanities might still fail to find any coherence in the whole; on the other hand, one with far more limited knowledge, by isolating within his range of knowledge certain basic notions and imaginatively experimenting in an effort to conceive alternatives to them, might have greater success. The metaphysician must check his formulations against the

[9]Whitehead, *op. cit.*, p. 14.
[10]Hartshorne, *Beyond Humanism* (Chicago: Willett, Clark & Company, 1937), p. 274.
[11]*Ibid.*

widest possible range of experience, but the fact that he can never have all possible experience does not render metaphysics impossible.

Commonsense objection to metaphysics can take a dozen different forms. For example, it may be said that the history of philosophy is simply a procession of metaphysical systems, no two of which are in agreement and no one of which is clearly the true one. Or it may be claimed that metaphysics has no practical importance, that we do not live by philosophical systems. In this connection common sense may assert that people manage to worship God without benefit of metaphysics, that religion is a matter of decision and commitment while metaphysics has no personal relevance or urgency. In general, the commonsense objection is that metaphysics is really pointless, that it gets us nowhere and is useless. Let us take the points raised and see how solid they are.

(1) It is true that the history of philosophy discloses a vast array of metaphysical systems. In itself this is no argument against metaphysics since a similar observation can be made about science and other disciplines respected by common sense. Lack of agreement among metaphysicians is no proof of a stalemate. Metaphysicians do not necessarily advance toward the truth single file; there are various ways of making progress, some of which may be more appropriate in metaphysics than continuous, unilinear development. Hartshorne observes that "the universal aspects of existence may not be discrete but may form a continuum. . . . It follows that there is no one final system of metaphysics, but an inexhaustible variety of ways of 'carving up' the ultimate continuum."[12] From this point of view progress in metaphysics would involve cutting the metaphysical pie in this way and that, according to the insights of individual philosophers. One metaphysician would see certain features of the world structure, a second would see others, and a third still others. Their differences would reflect the many-dimensionality in the nature of things.

---

[12]Hartshorne, *Philosophy of Science*, II, 291.

Metaphysicians also differ from one another for other reasons. For example, they differ because of their diverse powers of penetration. We need not suppose therefore that any given system is just as good as any other. Some system or other may very well be superior—and insofar be "the true one." But as Whitehead remarks, a system "is true with unformulated qualifications, exceptions, limitations, and new interpretations in terms of more general notions."[13] This suggests that a system may gain in adequacy (that is, in scope or comprehensiveness) if it is properly revised and refined. The systems of Plato, Aristotle, and other great metaphysicians are true in Whitehead's sense, and progress beyond them may consist in part in adjusting them. Even if we adopt an alternative which some thinker discarded, we are, as Whitehead says, nonetheless indebted to him.[14] Such a thinker has "gotten us somewhere" by enabling us to see the inadequacy of the path he took.

(2) To the objection that metaphysics has no practical importance, we may concede at once that it is not a technique for getting things done in the workaday world. But not everything valuable is useful *in this sense*. In discussing the question, "What's the use of the space program?" John Glenn, the first American astronaut to orbit the earth, recurred to Faraday's question: "What good is a baby?"[15] Both space exploration and babies are valuable; indeed, both have a kind of practical importance. Much the same can be said of metaphysics. Man's desire to understand is basic in his nature, and satisfaction of that desire is surely a self-justifying good.[16] Perhaps common sense will not deny the practical importance of satisfying basic desire. In any event, metaphysicians have no monopoly on the business of interpreting the world. As Whitehead says, "Our

---

[13]Whitehead, *op. cit.*, p. 13.

[14]Cf. *ibid.*, p. 16.

[15]See the editorial by William J. Coughlin, "What Good Is a Baby?" *Missiles and Rockets*, X (March, 1962), 54.

[16]This is not to deny that the method used to acquire understanding, or the circumstances under which it is acquired, may be evil. Nor is it to deny that understanding may be used for evil purposes.

habitual experience is a complex of failure and success in the enterprise of interpretation. If we desire a record of uninterpreted experience, we must ask a stone to record its autobiography."[17] Metaphysics is the attempt to achieve systematic and comprehensive interpretation of the world, and is therefore really the extension of a project which everyone in some sense carries on. It would not be going too far to say that the plain man always presupposes some rudimentary metaphysical principles. We do live by our philosophies, however naïve and unrefined they may be. Nor is this point refuted by the fact that a man may not be aware of his philosophical presuppositions. Millions of people have lived and died without knowing that they had lungs, kidneys, and a brain.

(3) The claim that people manage to worship God without benefit of metaphysics is true only in the sense that the worshiper need not have and often does not have a conscious conceptual system of the whole of things. But unless worship becomes a mere performance, it involves the conceptual equipment of the worshiper and ultimately his notions about the nature of things. Moreover, worship on its objective side is permeated by doctrinal elements which have metaphysical implications—as an examination of scriptures, creeds, prayers, sermons, and sacraments will disclose. A worshiper's metaphysical commitments may wholly escape his attention. If he is a layman, he may be pardoned for the oversight, but not if he is a theologian. To love God with the whole mind can mean nothing less than a sustained effort to apprehend and criticize one's intellectual underpinnings.

The theory that religion—in contrast to metaphysics—involves decision and commitment would not prove that metaphysics is irrelevant to religion. And since no one, so far as I know, is attempting to identify metaphysics and religion, the theory itself seems irrelevant. It does, however, furnish the opportunity to correct the misapprehension that metaphysicians are cold, blood-

---

[17]Whitehead, *op. cit.*, p. 22. Used by permission.

less creatures. Though he is disciplined, the metaphysician is not necessarily dispassionate. Though he is deliberate, he need not be detached. Passion has more than one form. It may rush headlong like a locomotive or patiently endure like a bridge. The metaphysician's passion takes the latter form. It sustains him over years of research and meditation. His task requires heart as well as mind.

His passion is directed toward a vision of the whole. Like Robert Frost's "something . . . that doesn't love a wall" and wants it down, the metaphysician is discontent with compartments. He seeks the integrity underlying all things, believing that the world is coherently structured, that man lives in a *uni*verse, not a *multi*verse.

CHAPTER II

A Split-Level Universe

> In the history of the human spirit I distinguish between
> epochs of habitation and epochs of homelessness. In the former,
> man lives in the world as in a house, as in a home. In the
> latter, man lives in the world as in an open field and at times
> does not even have four pegs with which to set up a tent.
>
> Martin Buber[1]

THE METAPHYSICIAN is like a man with binoculars who finds
that the two images, one from the right eyeglass, the other from
the left, do not easily fuse. With one eye the metaphysician
gazes at the calibrated world of science; with the other at the
vivid world of literature, history, fine art, religion, etc. Can the
two views be brought into a single focus so that each comple-
ments the other? The metaphysician, convinced that "the ultimate natures of things lie together in a harmony,"[2] faces here
a severe test, and his success in meeting this test is a measure of
his capacity as a metaphysician. The work of Alfred North
Whitehead (1861-1947) can be understood as an attempt to
bring science and the humanities into focus. In order to get some
idea of the problem of relating the two, we will examine the
formation of modern science and thereby be prepared to grasp
Whitehead's solution.

---

[1] From *Between Man and Man*, trans. Ronald Gregor Smith (New York: The
Macmillan Company, 1948), p. 126. Used by permission of Macmillan and Routledge
& Kegan Paul Ltd.

[2] Whitehead, *Science and the Modern World* (New York: The Macmillan Company,
1925), p. 27.

The year 1642—the date Galileo Galilei, the Italian physicist and astronomer, died and Isaac Newton, the British scientist, mathematician, and philosopher, was born—is the center of a 100-year period of scientific ferment and development. At the beginning of the period science had advanced little beyond Aristotle; at its close, the foundations of modern science had been firmly laid. We may tend to regard this achievement as a work of reason. It is certainly true that the founders of modern science believed in the order and intelligibility of nature (a belief with roots in medieval logic and the doctrine of divine providence as well as in Roman law and the Greek vision of fate). Kepler (German astronomer, 1571-1630), Galileo (1564-1642), and Descartes (French philosopher and mathematician, 1596-1650, who was preeminently a rationalist) held that mathematics can be used to unlock the secrets of nature. But the peculiarity of the emerging scientific mentality was its passion for facts, its attention to the details of natural occurrences. Scientific heads turned from medieval rationalism and devoted themselves to observation and experiment. The familiar allegation that a medieval man, if asked how many teeth a horse has, would try to argue his way to an answer or else consult Aristotle is doubtful. Yet it suggests something of the medieval temper and reminds us that it contrasts strikingly with that of modern science. The British historian Basil Willey cites the following illustration of the contrast.[3] The scholastics had argued that, unlike the earth, the heavenly bodies are unalterable and incorruptible, for they are subject only to circular motion, which has no contrary, and, as Aristotle said, an object is generated from its contrary and is corrupted back into its contrary. Galileo, desiring to show that the earth itself is one of the heavenly bodies, attacked this incorruptibility theory. His basic argument was that through his telescope he had seen generation and corruption occurring in the heavens. "The Professor of Philosophy

---

[3]See Basil Willey, *The Seventeenth Century Background* (London: Chatto & Windus, 1934), pp. 16-20.

at Padua," adds Willey, "refused to look through Galileo's telescope."[4]

The scientific genius of the seventeenth century produced a picture of the world which has prevailed until recent times. It is a picture constructed in terms of mass, distance, motion, time, and force. The world was seen as an infinite machine which could be understood only when its material and mechanism had been described. Doubtless this scientific picture of the world represents an achievement almost unrivaled in the history of Western thought. Operating within its framework, scientists have been eminently successful in their investigations of nature. But not all has been gain, for in a machine one can discover no purpose, no mind, no value, no life, no God. The scientific transformation of man's understanding of the world was drastic; indeed, it was staggering. Says E. A. Burtt:

> The gloriously romantic universe of Dante and Milton, that set no bounds to the imagination of man as it played over space and time, had now been swept away. Space was identified with the realm of geometry, time with the continuity of number. The world that people had thought themselves living in—a world rich with colour and sound, redolent with fragrance, filled with gladness, love and beauty, speaking everywhere of purposive harmony and creative ideals—was crowded now into minute corners in the brains of scattered organic beings. The really important world outside was a world hard, cold, colourless, silent, and dead; a world of quantity, a world of mathematically computable motions in mechanical regularity. The world of qualities as immediately perceived by man became just a curious and quite minor effect of that infinite machine beyond.[5]

Thus, the universe was split in two: there was the world outside, a world from which science had banished the things of the spirit; and there was the world inside, a world of thought, feeling, and perception. Descartes gave this split official status in philosophy. Reality, he said, is divided into extended substances (bodies) and thinking substances (minds), and neither type of

---

[4]*Ibid.*, p. 20.

[5]Edwin A. Burtt, *The Metaphysical Foundations of Modern Physical Science* (New York: Humanities Press, 1952), pp. 238-239. Used by permission.

substance involves the other in any way. Philosophy from Descartes forward has been powerfully influenced by the scientific scheme (which has usually been accepted at face value) and in particular by Descartes's dualistic rendering of it. Can the dualism of matter and mind be the last word? Is the universe, after all, split level?

If one adopts the scientific cosmology of Galileo and Newton (1642-1727), he is obliged also to adopt some form of Descartes's dualism—or deny altogether the reality of mind as distinct from matter. Descartes was not a thoroughgoing materialist: he held that the mind is an unextended, thinking spirit. His attempts to explain the relation of the mind to the body were never really clear. Burtt comments that "the net result of his [Descartes's] attempts on this point for the positive scientific current of thought was that the mind existed in a ventricle of the brain."[6] By the end of the seventeenth century, almost all educated people conceived the mind as imprisoned within the brain, occupying a seat known as the sensorium. The important point, however, is that man as a psychic being had been exiled from nature. His purposes and feelings, his thoughts and ideals, were wholly alien to its clocklike mechanism.

A minister who warns against materialism is very likely referring to the lust for goods and gadgets. But is the materialism which views the physical world as mere dead stuff any less a foe, from the religious viewpoint? And isn't it true that most men still subscribe to the materialistic cosmology despite the radically new situation in present-day physical science? (There is an explanation for their subscribing to it, as we shall see.) To one who believes that stars, planets, oceans, skies, animals, plants, and even his own body are forms of lifeless matter, the claim that the universe is religiously meaningful will have a hollow ring—even if he himself makes this claim. It requires little insight to see that such materialism oppresses the spirit. Scientists in the seventeenth century were often awed by the

---

[6]*Ibid.*, p. 123. Used by permission.

mathematical majesty of the world machine. But a machine is no home for the human spirit—as Blaise Pascal (1623-1662) recognized.[7] In the Middle Ages man had been at home in his world. Now his bond with the world had been dissolved, and he found himself amid swirling, heedless chunks and bits of matter. He had become a stranger in the world; he was no longer secure. Nor have succeeding centuries restored man's sense of the world as a home. Today we may admit little if any nostalgia about a lost unity with the world, but our attitudes toward nature betray our estrangement from her, and our homelessness. We speak of the world as an aggregation of objects—things which have weight and occupy space, things to be manipulated and used. It strikes most of us as strange when Martin Buber, the eminent Jewish philosopher, speaks of an "I—Thou" meeting with a horse, a cat, or a tree. We are concerned with the control of nature, and even with her conquest and exploitation. To be sure, poets, artists, and philosophers have all along protested against the new, scientific version of nature and man's relation to it. But such protests have had little effect, and men, grown accustomed to their exile from nature, have accepted the split-level universe of Descartes.

I am neither damning science nor pleading for a return to the Middle Ages. I am questioning whether science can give a full, concrete reading of things. So long as one sticks to certain types of facts, science is no doubt a superb instrument of interpretation. But how exhaustive is scientific interpretation? Are there not features of the universe which can be grasped or expressed only nonscientifically? If so, the scientific scheme is an abstraction, a partial truth, a simplified edition of things. "I hold that philosophy is the critic of abstractions," says Whitehead. "Its function is the double one, first of harmonising them by assigning

---

[7]Martin Buber remarks: "Pascal, a great scientist, a mathematician and a physicist, young and destined to die early, experienced beneath the starry heavens not merely, as Kant did, their majesty, but still more powerfully their uncanniness: *le silence éternel de ces espaces infinis m'effraie*. [The eternal silence of these infinite spaces frightens me.]" Buber, *Between Man and Man*, p. 131. Used by permission. The quotation from Pascal is found in *Les Pensées*, Section III, 206.

to them their right relative status as abstractions, and secondly of *completing them by direct comparison with more concrete intuitions of the universe,* and thereby promoting the formation of more complete schemes of thought."[8] Thus, if science is abstract —and Whitehead insists that it is—the philosopher (metaphysician) must bring it into relation with more concrete intuitions. The testimony of the man of letters is no less important than that of the scientist. Their respective intuitions must be synthesized; as we said, they must like binocular images be fused. "It is in respect to this comparison [of abstractions with more concrete intuitions] that the testimony of great poets is of such importance,"[9] Whitehead observes. Because Wordsworth insisted that the important facts of nature elude scientific method, he was a poet of special interest to Whitehead. During the years that Whitehead and Bertrand Russell (1872-   ) were collaborating on their monumental *Principia Mathematica* (a highly technical work in logic and mathematics) Whitehead would in the evenings pore over Wordsworth's lines as over a scientific treatise. Years later, in the first of the books Whitehead published after moving to the United States, he included a chapter called "The Romantic Reaction" in which he quoted from Wordsworth's *The Prelude* and then remarked as follows:

In thus citing Wordsworth, the point which I wish to make is that we forget how strained and paradoxical is the view of nature which modern science imposes on our thoughts. Wordsworth, to the height of genius, expresses the concrete facts of our apprehension, facts which are distorted in the scientific analysis. Is it not possible that the standardised concepts of science are only valid within narrow limitations, perhaps too narrow for science itself?[10]

What exactly is "the view of nature which modern science imposes on our thoughts"? Heretofore we have spoken of it only

---

[8]Reprinted with permission of the publisher from *Science and the Modern World,* by Alfred North Whitehead. Copyright 1925, The Macmillan Company, p. 126. Renewed 1953 by Evelyn Whitehead. Also by permission of Cambridge University Press. Italics added.

[9]*Ibid.*

[10]*Ibid.*, p. 122. Reprinted with permission.

in general terms; suppose we try to fill in some details, particularly in regard to its origin and basis. Whitehead points out that the scientific giants of the sixteenth and seventeenth centuries worked from a set of commonsense assumptions.[11] They were the same assumptions which even today we find quite natural and obvious, and seldom question. Thus, we ordinarily imagine the world to be an aggregate of material things which are relatively permanent—though capable of moving about in empty space. "There are chairs, tables, bits of rock, oceans, animal bodies, vegetable bodies, planets, and suns."[12] The passage of time doesn't make the slightest difference to any of these things. A chair, for example, is simply itself whether we take it at an instant or over a stretch of time. In addition, each object has a set of qualities such as color, smell, and shape; and changes in these qualities make up the events of nature. Locomotion is one of the more important of these qualities, since objects are connected solely by spatial relations. By walking down the street a man changes his spatial relation to all other objects and likewise theirs to him. The geometer studies the laws of space, that universal receptacle which is everywhere homogeneous and forever changeless.

This commonsense characterization of nature furnished the terms in which the founders of modern science tried to answer all their questions. One of the foremost questions was: what are the laws of motion? Sir Isaac Newton, who was one of Whitehead's predecessors at Trinity College, Cambridge, formulated three laws of motion, which have proved basic in modern physics, and in his famous law of universal gravitation specified the precise manner in which any two bodies attract one another. Nowadays every school child has heard of Newton and his great law of gravitation. Actually, the discovery of the laws of motion and even of the law of gravitation began with Galileo, who was obliged to argue against the venerable Aristotelian tra-

[11]See Whitehead, *Modes of Thought* (New York: The Macmillan Company, 1938), pp. 175-176.
[12]*Ibid.*, p. 174.

dition (a course of action for which he was condemned by the church). Centuries earlier Aristotle had concluded that a body will remain at rest unless it is pushed along by an outside force. The facts of everyday experience plainly support this conclusion. Anyone who has tried to budge an old piano knows how dogged a body can be about staying put. And does not a moving body always come to rest? When a golfer tees off, he does not doubt that his ball will stop somewhere—though he may have considerable doubt as to the exact spot. Galileo, however, saw that a moving body comes to rest only because various forces compel it to do so; that in the absence of forces acting on the moving body, it would continue to move uniformly in a straight line. Here was a breakthrough, one that put the science of dynamics on a completely new basis. For two thousand years Aristotle's doctrine of motion had prevailed, and accordingly men had searched for forces *sustaining* the motion of bodies. Galileo saw that there is no need to invoke outside forces to explain the motion of a body so long as it maintains the same speed and direction. It is rather the *changes* in speed or direction that need explanation and that such outside forces explain. Thus, while Kepler, following Aristotle, had looked for forces pushing the planets about in their orbits, Newton, following Galileo, looked for forces diverting them from motion in a straight line (and found the required forces in the gravitational pull of the sun). The new Galilean conception of motion was expressed by Newton as the first law of motion. Referring to this law, Whitehead says:

This is the first article of the creed of science; and like the Church's creeds it is more than a mere statement of belief: it is a pæan of triumph over defeated heretics [the Aristotelians]. It should be set to music and chanted in the halls of Universities.[13]

Galileo almost stumbled upon the doctrine of universal gravitation. Unlike the Aristotelians, who taught that different parts

---

[13]Whitehead, *Science and Philosophy* (New York: Philosophical Library, Inc., 1948), p. 245. Used by permission.

of nature function in entirely different ways (for example, that earth and water move toward the center of the universe, air and fire toward the moon), Galileo held that each of the heavenly bodies (which move in an indifferent, neutral space) attracts its various parts into harmonious unity. He was thinking of the earth, the sun, the moon, etc. "His guardian angel," says Whitehead, "does not appear to have whispered to him the generalization, '*any* material body.' "[14] The distinction of having grasped that generalization belongs to Newton. According to legend, the idea occurred to him after he had watched an apple fall to earth. In any event, he was doubtless aided by Galileo's theory about the unity of a heavenly body. With this point in mind Whitehead suggests that at the moment of discovery Newton's train of thought may have run something like this:

"What are the Earth and the Sun and the Moon? Why, they are any bodies! We should say therefore that any bodies attract. But if this be the case, the Earth and the Sun and the Moon attract each other, and we have the cause maintaining the planets in their orbits."[15]

The final generalization had been reached. Each thing attracts every other thing—the earth the apple and the apple the earth. Now the task was to find a way of measuring the attraction between two bodies. Newton had found that the magnitude of a force acting on a body can be determined by multiplying the mass of the body by its acceleration. On the basis of this conception, he proceeded to show that the magnitude of such a force can also be determined by taking account of the masses of the bodies involved and the distance between them.[16] Newton had presented to the world the law of gravitation.

These technicalities are sufficient to show that physicists had adopted the commonsense view of the world. Indeed, no one thought of putting things in any other way. It was just taken

---

[14]*Ibid.*, p. 243. Italics added.

[15]*Ibid.*, p. 244. Used by permission.

[16]Two bodies attract each other with a force proportional to the product of their masses and inversely proportional to the square of the distance between them.

for granted that the world is made up of material parts, which are simply here or there in space and time, requiring for their explanation no reference beyond themselves. Whitehead calls this the doctrine of simple location, and he spells it out like this:

Each stone is conceived as fully describable apart from any reference to any other portion of matter. It might be alone in the Universe, the sole occupant of uniform space. But it would still be that stone which it is. Also the stone could be adequately described without any reference to past or future. It is to be conceived fully and adequately as wholly constituted within the present moment.[17]

A corollary of this doctrine is the theory that an object is a substance in which various qualities inhere. For example, we may come across an object which is round, damp, white, and cold. We say these are "its" qualities—despite the fact that observation never reveals anything *except* qualities. Thus, we regard the qualities as *belonging to the object,* which supports them much as an unseen foundation supports a house. In addition, we distinguish essential qualities (apart from which the object would not be itself) from nonessential or accidental qualities (which may change without affecting the definition of the object).

The development of natural science from the seventeenth century to the present has required the abandonment of every item in the commonsense picture. Paradoxically, the initial steps in this process were taken by the seventeenth-century scientists themselves. Of course, they probably had little intention of forsaking any of their commonsense presuppositions, since they were scarcely conscious of them. Nonetheless, the swift current of their thought began the erosion of those presuppositions.

(1) The first to be called into question was the theory of sense qualities. The great Dutch physicist Christian Huyghens (1629-1695) held that light is transmitted by waves of ether (a

---

[17]Reprinted with permission of the publisher from *Adventures of Ideas* by Alfred North Whitehead. Copyright 1933, The Macmillan Company, pp. 200-201. Renewed 1961 by Evelyn Whitehead. Also by permission of Cambridge University Press.

spooky kind of matter), while Newton held that it is transmitted by tiny corpuscles of rarefied matter. But observe: on neither theory can it be maintained that light or color actually belong to the external world. Nothing is "out there" except matter in motion, whose impingement on the optical apparatus produces in us the sensations we call light and color. Likewise, the theory that sound is transmitted to the ear by air waves yields the conclusion that external nature is completely soundless. Analogous reasoning applies to smell, taste, etc. As Galileo, Descartes, Newton, Locke,[18] and others maintained, all such qualities are "secondary"—that is, they arise in the mind in response to physical stimulation of the sense organs, nerves, and brain. By contrast, "primary qualities" are resident in the external world. Among these are figure, magnitude, motion, and number.[19] This doctrine of primary and secondary qualities represents a drastic revision of the commonsense view. It is based on the distinction between matter and mind, a distinction Descartes interpreted dualistically, as we have seen. According to Whitehead, Descartes's dualism rests on an error, for it assumes that the scientific scheme presents the full, concrete facts about the external world. (Thus, it mistakes the abstract for the concrete and thereby commits what Whitehead calls the "Fallacy of Misplaced Concreteness.") On the other hand, Whitehead is no advocate of the commonsense doctrine of sense qualities. He agrees with the seventeenth-century scientists that to associate a sense quality such as color, sound, or smell

---

[18]John Locke (1632-1704), an Englishman, was a physician by profession, but he is remembered as one of Britain's greatest philosophers.

[19]In explaining the doctrine of primary and secondary qualities, Whitehead uses the following excellent example: "Suppose we look at Westminster Abbey. It has been standing there, grey and immovable, for centuries past. But, according to modern scientific theory, that greyness, which so heightens our sense of the immobility of the building, is itself nothing but our way of appreciating the rapid motions of the ultimate molecules, which form the outer surface of the building and communicate vibrations to a substance called the ether. Again we lay our hands on its stones and note their cool, even temperature, so symbolic of the quiet repose of the building. But this feeling of temperature simply marks our sense of the transfer of heat from the hand to the stone, or from the stone to the hand; and, according to modern science, heat is nothing but the agitation of the molecules of a body. Finally, the organ begins playing, and again sound is nothing but the result of motions of the air striking on the drum of the ear." Alfred North Whitehead, *An Introduction to Mathematics* (New York: Oxford University Press, 1948), p. 31. Used by permission.

with an external object is an artificial procedure. "Sense-perception," he says, "for all its practical importance is very superficial in its disclosure of the nature of things."[20]

(2) Science has gradually abandoned the commonsense notion that objects are moving in empty space. The attack on this notion began in the seventeenth century with the very men who discredited the commonsense doctrine of sense qualities. According to the transmission theories of light and sound mentioned above, space is to be conceived as full rather than empty. Furthermore, Newton had proclaimed that the motion of a body is conditioned by its spatial relations to other bodies, and such conditioning is sheer mystery if the body is moving in empty space. Subsequently, science has completely replaced the theory of empty space. In the nineteenth century, scientists held that ether permeates space. While it was regarded as ordinary matter, ether was thought to have the properties of a jelly. Perceptible objects were supposed to be "knots in the ether,"[21] which impose stresses and strains throughout the jellylike medium and transmit their own agitations as agitations of these stresses and strains. In this century, the whole of space came to be conceived as "a field of force, or in other words, a field of incessant activity."[22] Thus, the empty space of common sense has been eliminated from scientific thought.

(3) Recent science has discarded the everyday concept of matter, largely as the result of the study of ether, for upon examination the activities of ether were found to be quite different from those ordinarily ascribed to matter. Indeed, "matter" could be understood merely as the appearance presented by certain activities of ether. The doctrine of simple location was at stake. It has been swept away completely by the twentieth-century revolution in physics. Says Whitehead: "Matter has

---

[20]Whitehead, *Modes of Thought*, p. 181.
[21]*Ibid.*, pp. 186-187.
[22]*Ibid.*, p. 186.

been identified with energy, and energy is sheer activity."[23] According to the modern point of view, then, ordinary matter is a group of agitations, which is fused into the environment. Some general, average features of such a group may remain more or less stable. But the fundamental fact is that the ever-changing environment flows into the group-agitation, which in turn penetrates the environment. Indeed, the universe is in a sense a single, complex state of activity. We may, of course, isolate a certain set of activities and study the interrelations within that set, but any such abstraction ignores connections with the whole system of activities.

Despite its official dethronement, the old commonsense view still prevails in ordinary life; indeed, in some measure it prevails even in science. This means that the doctrines of matter (with simple location) and substance (with qualities) continue to inform—or better, misinform—the modern mind even as they did the mind of the seventeenth century. As a matter of fact, the Newtonian world picture, with its dualism of matter and mind, still hangs on doggedly. The reason for this is simply that it is based on the commonsense view, which is so natural and obvious to us. Thus, the new wine of science is often poured into old wineskins, and the result, as Whitehead observes, is a muddle in both science and philosophy.[24]

The modern world has been an epoch of homelessness for the human spirit, an epoch during which materialism has enjoyed an unprecedented and almost unchallenged reign. But to Whitehead the notion that the universe is a vast machine— "soundless, scentless, colourless; merely the hurrying of material, endlessly, meaninglessly"[25]—is quite unbelievable. "This conception of the universe is surely framed in terms of high abstractions," he insists, "and the paradox [this unbelievable conception of the universe] only arises because we have mistaken our

---

[23]*Ibid.*, p. 188.
[24]See *ibid.*, p. 180.
[25]Whitehead, *Science and the Modern World*, p. 80.

abstraction for concrete realities."[26] Whitehead gladly accepts the point of view of recent physics in which process, activity, and change are seen as fundamental. But he is not satisfied to leave things there. Though he is a scientist, he is concerned with the total range of experience. "How do we add content to the notion of bare activity?"[27] he asks. This question is vital to anyone concerned with beauty, value, purpose, life, or God— in short, with the things of the spirit. Can the world of process, activity, and change—the world of present-day physics—be conceived more fully and completely, more concretely? If so, perhaps science and the humanities, with their diverse outlooks, can be reconciled. The matter is of first importance to the metaphysician, who seeks to see life steadily and whole. Whitehead, the greatest metaphysician of our century, undertakes to conceive the natural world in its concreteness; he sees it not as a machine but as a society whose members are alive. In the following chapter we will examine his conception and the evidence on which it rests.

---

[26]*Ibid.*, pp. 80-81.
[27]Whitehead, *Modes of Thought*, pp. 200-201.

CHAPTER III

The Two Shall Become One

The doctrine that I am maintaining is that neither physical nature nor life can be understood unless we fuse them together.
Alfred North Whitehead, in *Modes of Thought*

A DOZEN YEARS have passed since my copy of Whitehead's *Process and Reality* arrived in the mail. It is a difficult book, and I have pored over its pages time and again. First published in 1929, it sets forth Whitehead's entire system. In addition to *Process and Reality,* his metaphysical works include *Science and the Modern World* (1925), *Adventures of Ideas* (1933), and *Modes of Thought* (1938). It is not possible in a book of this length to do full justice to Whitehead's metaphysics. Indeed, I will be able to provide only the scantiest outline or (more precisely) impression of his thought.

Most people educated in this country are deeply influenced by the method and doctrines of science, whether directly or indirectly. If they are Christians, they may have difficulty reconciling their religious convictions with scientific teaching or its implications. They may not be troubled by the difficulties usually recited under the heading of conflict between science and religion. Many Christians have made their peace with evolution and other scientific doctrines, and willingly admit that the significance of the Bible does not depend on interpreting it literally. Some, however, are bothered by the tendency found among scientists to explain everything *solely* in terms of chemical or physical processes. What they find objectionable is the claim that science can account for the entire range of experience.

Whitehead is one of those rare geniuses who are at home not only in science and mathematics but also in history, literature, art, philosophy, religion, and to some extent politics and business. By presenting a vision of the world in which Descartes's dualism of matter and mind is overcome, Whitehead sheds light on how religion and science can be brought into rapport with one another. I am far from suggesting that religion is just one of the humanities, which must somehow be brought into relation with science. Religion is far more than an academic discipline; it is a total way of life. But religion suffocates in the atmosphere of scientific materialism, and a metaphysics in which the world (in its concreteness) is viewed as a society whose members are alive will be congenial to the man of religion—as well as to the poet, the artist, the historian, and others.

Whitehead's life belongs to two centuries and to two countries.[1] He was born in England during the twenty-fourth year of Queen Victoria's lengthy reign. There he was educated, and there he distinguished himself as a mathematician and scientist, first in Cambridge and then in London. On reaching the age of retirement in 1924, Whitehead came to the United States to be professor of philosophy at Harvard. Thus he embarked on a new career in a new land. During his years here, his metaphysical works appeared—each of them brilliant and original, providing mines of thought for centuries to come. Whitehead became Professor Emeritus after thirteen years of teaching at Harvard. He continued to live in Cambridge, Massachusetts, until his death in 1947 at the age of eighty-six.

---

[1] The following account is based largely upon Whitehead's "Autobiographical Notes" in *Science and Philosophy*. I have also made use of *Dialogues of Alfred North Whitehead* (as recorded by Lucien Price) (Boston: Little, Brown and Company, 1954).

Doubtless, the fruition of a life owes much to its beginning. Back of the man Whitehead and his towering achievements is the boy of the parsonage at Ramsgate, England. Here, on February 15, 1861, Alfred North Whitehead was born. Ramsgate, one of the little seaports along the white chalk cliffs of Kent in southeast England, faces the North Sea at its junction with the English Channel. The Narrow Seas, Whitehead observes, have impressed their character on the coastal populations, instilling in them the characteristics of obstinacy and a tendency to lonely thought.[2]

Whitehead's father, after eight years as a schoolmaster in Ramsgate, was ordained an Anglican clergyman in 1860 but did not give up his school until 1866 or 1867, when he began clerical service in Ramsgate. In 1871 he was appointed Vicar of St. Peter's Parish, a district whose church was two or three miles from Ramsgate. While it is certainly true, as Charles Hartshorne says, that Whitehead's philosophy requires a doctrine of God,[3] it would be unwise to discount the influence of a clergyman father on the mind of young Whitehead, who until his fourteenth year remained at home and was taught by his father. Whitehead has vivid memories of his father and the clergy of East Kent. He refers to his father as an Old Testament man, who possessed the fervor of the prophets and a voice that resounded mightily beneath the barrel vault of his old Norman church. As a lad Whitehead often went along on his father's daily visits to each of his three parochial schools. Tait, the Archbishop of Canterbury, was a close friend of Whitehead's parents, and Whitehead counted the Archbishop as one of the few great men he had met.[4]

I have always been grateful for my glimpse of him during half-a-dozen years, and for the family tradition of him during a longer period. To have seen Tait was worth shelves of volumes of mediæval history.[5]

[2]See Whitehead, *Science and Philosophy*, p. 47.
[3]See Charles Hartshorne and William L. Reese, *Philosophers Speak of God* (Chicago: The University of Chicago Press, 1953), p. 273.
[4]See Whitehead, *Science and Philosophy*, p. 27.
[5]*Ibid.*, p. 28. Used by permission.

I have said that in his metaphysics Whitehead seeks to integrate the scientific view with that of the humanities. His interest in the humanities was awakened in his earliest years. "History for this lad was not something learned out of a book," says Lucien Price of Whitehead; "he rubbed elbows with it every day and took it in at eyes and nostrils."[6] Sixteen miles to the west of Ramsgate is Canterbury Cathedral, where a visitor may see the very stone on which Thomas à Becket was felled in 1170, or view the armor of Edward, the Black Prince, who died in 1376. Southwest of Whitehead's birthplace, and somewhat closer than Canterbury, stand the massive walls of Richborough Castle, the silent remains of an old Roman fortress. South of Ramsgate is the beach where the Saxons landed; on that same beach Augustine of Canterbury landed in 597, one hundred and fifty years after the Saxons. The village of Minster, a mile or so to the west of Ramsgate, marks the spot where Augustine first preached Christianity to Ethelbert, king of Kent. Of all the old Norman churches scattered about this corner of Kent, the finest is the Abbey Church at Minster, set amidst the relics of a once-important monastery.

Not only from the historical remains which surrounded his boyhood home, but in other ways and places Whitehead absorbed his rich cultural heritage. In the 1860's he used to spend two months each spring with his grandmother in London. Standing at a window in her house, the boy Alfred Whitehead could look across Green Park toward Buckingham Palace. To his eyes Queen Victoria—"a little figure in black, belonging to the unquestioned order of the universe"[7]—was a familiar sight, for he often saw her pass by in her carriage. At the age of six Whitehead was introduced to his first novel (Dickens' *Pickwick Papers*) by his grandmother's housemaid, who read aloud to him by the hour. Whitehead remarks that *Pickwick* gave him his first insight into the English social system. His early schooling in-

---

[6]*Dialogues of Alfred North Whitehead*, p. 4.
[7]Whitehead, *Science and Philosophy*, p. 23.

cluded work in history, language, and the classics. He had already learned the rudiments of Greek and Latin from his father when at age fourteen he was sent to school at Sherborne in Dorsetshire. The school had been founded by Saint Aldhelm and in 1941 celebrated its twelve-hundredth anniversary. Here, under the sound of the great bells of the Abbey Church, Whitehead continued his study of Greek and Latin (the Bible was read only in Greek) and learned history by way of the Greek and Roman historians. "The Greeks reigned supreme in our minds,"[8] says Whitehead, reflecting on those years. A little mathematics, some science and French, and a few Shakespearian plays rounded out his classical education in those late years of the 1870's. Excused from some work on Latin poetry so that he could have more time for mathematics, young Whitehead nonetheless spent his spare time reading poetry (especially Wordsworth and Shelley) and history, both of which had become major interests to him. Thus, even this early stage of Whitehead's life reveals his two great devotions, the one to science, the other to the humanities.

Whitehead entered Trinity College, Cambridge, in 1880 at the age of nineteen. Since his undergraduate work there was entirely in mathematics, we might assume that any concern he had had for literature and history soon withered away. And perhaps it would have, had it not been for the continual stimulus of discussion outside the lecture hall. "At Cambridge," says Whitehead, "what civilization we got, came from outside."[9] Each evening there was conversation with fellow undergraduates or staff members, beginning at dinner and continuing for two or three hours. Every topic was aired: "politics, religion, philosophy, literature—with a bias toward literature."[10] In addition, Whitehead was a member of "The Apostles," a group of men who met for discussion on Saturday nights at ten o'clock. He regarded the club, which had been started by Tennyson and his

---

[8]*Ibid.*, p. 42.
[9]*Dialogues of Alfred North Whitehead,* p. 354.
[10]Whitehead, *Science and Philosophy,* p. 13.

friends in the late 1820's, as an important influence in his life. It helped provide a precious balance and contrast for the intensive work he was doing in mathematics.

In 1885, at the age of twenty-four, Whitehead took—and passed—his examinations for a fellowship at Trinity. Having taken the exams as a shot in the dark, he had entertained little hope of receiving the fellowship and so had gone away for the summer without even leaving an address. "With additional luck," Whitehead comments modestly, "a teaching job was added."[11] He continued teaching at Cambridge for thirty years, resigning his position as Senior Lecturer in mathematics in 1910. At the close of his first decade at Cambridge, he married Evelyn Wade, who though Irish had been born and reared in France and had come to England as a girl of seventeen. Her effect on his outlook was profound. Looking back, he observes: "Her vivid life has taught me that beauty, moral and æsthetic, is the aim of existence."[12] Such an outlook "directs attention to the periods of great art and literature, as best expressing the essential values of life."[13] Thus, one may judge that the "vivid life" of Mrs. Whitehead effectively tempered the high abstractions of her mathematician husband.

Whitehead's was evidently no one-track mind. While he was a mathematician by profession, he was at home with the works of men of letters, poets, and historians. Furthermore, he was involved in administration and politics. Even as a schoolboy at Sherborne, he had had responsibility for keeping order in the dormitory; on one occasion he had found it necessary to cane a boy who was guilty of stealing. While at Cambridge, Whitehead was in the middle of considerable political and academic controversy, a burning question of the day being the emancipation of women. He did a good bit of political speaking in country villages of the district. "Rotten eggs and oranges were

[11]*Ibid.*, p. 14.
[12]*Ibid.*, p. 15.
[13]*Ibid.*

48

effective party weapons, and I have often been covered by them,"[14] he remarks. On leaving Cambridge, Whitehead moved to London, where he managed to combine a heavy schedule of administrative and committee work with his teaching. The experience broadened and deepened his relations with the practical side of education. In addition, it opened his eyes to the problems of higher education in a modern industrial society, where people of every age and class seek enlightenment. Later he expressed the conviction that the more theoretical side of university studies should maintain close contact with the professional schools (law, business, medicine, theology, and the like). "It is midsummer madness on the part of universities to withdraw themselves from the closest contact with vocational practices,"[15] he insists.

For a year after his move to London in the summer of 1910, Whitehead held no academic position, but from 1911 to 1914 he served in several capacities at University College. In 1914 he secured a professorship at the Imperial College of Science and Technology in Kensington. Here he remained until 1924 when he accepted an invitation to become professor of philosophy at Harvard.

If Whitehead's capacity for practical activities, both in Cambridge and in London, was impressive, his academic output in these places was spectacular. His first book, *A Treatise on Universal Algebra,* was published in 1898 when he was thirty-seven. It led to his election to the Royal Society (1903). Whitehead collaborated with his former student Bertrand Russell for some nine years in writing the three-volume *Principia Mathematica* (published 1910-1913). During his decade at the Imperial College, Whitehead's fertile, probing mind shifted its focus. He now sought to work out a philosophy of nature and published three significant works in this area from 1919 to 1922. Ultimately, at Harvard, his philosophical thought expanded into a full-scale

---

[14]*Ibid.,* p. 20.
[15]*Ibid.,* p. 232.

theory of reality, one so vast, original, and profound as to challenge and inspire the keenest of minds.

The invitation to join the Harvard faculty came to Whitehead at age sixty-three. "I would rather do that than anything in the world,"[16] said Whitehead. At the end of August, 1924, he and his wife steamed into Boston harbor to begin their new life in the United States. During his thirteen years of teaching at Harvard, Whitehead published eight books in philosophy. His last book *(Modes of Thought)* was published in 1938, the year after his retirement. Whitehead observes that nearly thirty years after his election to the Royal Society (1903), he received the fellowship of the British Academy for his work in philosophy (1931). These two events, almost thirty years apart, measure the steady expansion of his mind from mathematics to philosophy of nature and finally to metaphysics. In each area, Whitehead exhibited creative genius.

Whitehead's life and career demonstrate that he was anything but a narrow specialist. Sensitive to the whole spectrum of human culture, he could not possibly accept scientific materialism at face value. By the turn of the century the Newtonian scheme had been officially overthrown. And yet, as we observed in the last chapter, the materialistic interpretation has never been completely shaken off. Even when nature is interpreted in the terms supplied by the new physics—that is, in terms of process, activity, and change—a split between nature and mind remains. It is as though there were two distinct worlds: one consisting of invisible, jitterbugging energy particles whose mass movements can be charted statistically; the other consisting of emotions, enjoyments, valuations of alternatives, decisions, and the like. Science, which limits itself to the former, omits from its picture of nature the very features which are basic in human experience. As Whitehead remarks, "Scientific reasoning is completely dominated by the presupposition that mental functionings are not properly part of nature."[17] It is quite all right to adopt such

---

[16]*Dialogues of Alfred North Whitehead,* p. 10.
[17]Whitehead, *Modes of Thought,* pp. 213-214.

a notion as a matter of procedure. But in the final analysis nature apart from life is simply unintelligible. "It cannot be that these [the activities of nature] are merely the formulae of the multiplication table—in the words of a great philosopher, merely a bloodless dance of categories."[18] Content must be added to the formulae if nature is to be conceived in its full-blooded concreteness. How do we add this content? According to Whitehead, it can be done only by fusing nature and life. Thus, the two shall become one, and the outlook of science will be joined with that of the humanities. No man was better equipped to carry out the proposed synthesis than Whitehead. His entire life was preparation for the task of criticizing abstractions and giving a unified interpretation of the world.

The claim that nature and life must be fused sounds preposterous. Can Whitehead be suggesting that all nature is somehow animated? Is he just a starry-eyed visionary? A correct answer demands that we keep firmly in mind that his basic intention is to give a fully understandable account of things. If we take the findings of modern science as the complete picture of nature, we mistake the abstract for the concrete—much as a man would if he mistook the menu for the meal. An abstraction is only a slice of reality; it is never the whole story, for it omits connections with the whole. The philosopher—indeed, the reasonable man—will seek those connections. This suggests that aesthetic intuitions are fully as relevant to the interpretation of nature as are the formulae of science. The divorce of life from nature, a divorce instigated in modern philosophy by Descartes, is intolerable as a fundamental characterization of things. What Descartes put asunder, Whitehead joins together. The two—nature and life—shall become one.

Basically, says Whitehead, "life" involves sheer enjoyment, enjoyment valuable in and of itself. He conceives an experience as a complex process in which data given by the past are brought into aesthetic synthesis in the present. The

---

[18]*Ibid.*, p. 197. The philosopher referred to is the Englishman F. H. Bradley.

process is not just a rearranging of past data. It involves elements of novelty and accordingly the realization of previously unactualized possibilities. The entire process is guided by its aim at enjoying the data in a particular way, selected from the range of unactualized possibilities. Enjoyment belongs not to any static result of the process but to the entire process.

Leaving aside the details of Whitehead's analysis, we can see that his basic point is this: the characteristics of life (aim, creativity, and enjoyment) belong in some sense to each of the really real things comprising the universe. We have every right to demand that our philosopher show how experience supports this conception.

If we look at the world around us, what we see are simply colored regions, some of which may be moving about or even changing in color. In any event, they give no hint of life anywhere. Yet, as Whitehead points out, this account of our seeing the world neglects a fundamental consideration. For as we look at things we are directly aware (though not always fully conscious) of seeing *with our eyes*. Indeed, all modes of sense perception—sight, hearing, taste, smell, and touch—exhibit this curious hybrid character: on the one hand, there are the data, perceived as yonder in the external world; on the other hand, there are the obscure bodily feelings, composing a background for the perceptual experience. Bodily reference is more prominent in some modes of sense perception than in others.

In the case of sight, the irrelevance to the body is at its maximum. We look at the scenery, at a picture, or at an approaching car on the road, as an external presentation given for our mental entertainment or mental anxiety.[19]

Nonetheless, bodily reference, though recessive, is present, and on reflection we can usually dredge up the fact that we have been seeing with our eyes. In addition, experiments show that it is the physiological functioning of our bodies that determines

---

[19]*Ibid.*, p. 209. Used by permission of The Macmillan Company and Cambridge University Press.

what we see and where we see it. In the other modes of perception dependence on the body is even more extensive.

Therefore, when we ask Whitehead how experience supports his doctrine that nature is alive, he replies that we must first consider what constitutes an experience of nature. Thereupon he calls to our attention the fact that sense perception is actually the product of the functioning of our own bodies. "Thus if we wish to understand the relation of our personal experience to the activities of nature, the proper procedure is to examine the dependence of our personal experiences upon our personal bodies."[20] Whitehead's point will be clearer if we keep in mind not only (1) the unity of personal experience with the body but also (2) the unity of the body with nature. We always presuppose unity with our bodies: never would anyone suppose that his body is not part of himself. If, for example, a wasp stings my finger, I do not hesitate to affirm that *I* have been stung. So fundamental is the persuasion concerning the unity of mind and body that it is a little surprising to find philosophers neglecting bodily reference in their theories of knowledge and treating man as a disembodied intellect. Whitehead says that while the functioning of the body produces sense experience, its total contribution to personal experience is far greater. The healthy functioning of the heart, lungs, bowels, kidneys, etc., gives rise to an emotional state of well-being. The derivation of emotion from one's own body underlies his sense of unity with the body.

It is no less true that the body is unified with nature. "In fact," says Whitehead, "it is just as much part of nature as anything else there—a river, or a mountain, or a cloud."[21] No exact boundary between body and environment can be drawn, for the body is continually gaining and losing molecules in an indefinite number of ways. Nor could the body survive in isolation from the environment. The double fact—that personal

---

[20]*Ibid.*, p. 218. Used by permission.
[21]*Ibid.*, p. 30.

experience is unified with the body and the body with nature—implies that bodily feelings, however vague, constitute our primary contact with nature.

Is nature alive? Well, if we merely gaze around we may find little or nothing to suggest an affirmative answer. But if we recognize that our own bodily feelings give us a direct, intimate disclosure of nature, an affirmative answer is unavoidable. One fundamental characteristic of personal experience—in addition to its derivation from the body—has yet to be mentioned, namely, its flow from the past into the present. Our experience in the present issues from our immediately preceding state of mind.

A quarter of a second ago, we were entertaining such and such ideas, we were enjoying such and such emotions, and we were making such and such observations of external fact. In our present state of mind, we are continuing that previous state.[22]

Indeed, we have a tendency to *identify* ourselves with the previous state. The truth is that the functionings of our bodies have introduced new elements, which have fused with our most recent experiences. Thereby the previous state has been modified, however slightly.

Whitehead is trying to cut beneath the abstractions in terms of which human experience is ordinarily described. Our experience, he contends, is a unity of data derived from the body and from the immediately past state of mind. The data are knit together by virtue of the fact that each of them receives a place in a pattern of feeling. The unity of the data, therefore, is a felt unity. It is a new creation, constituting the very being of the person in the present; yet, there is no break with the past. An experience may, from the point of view of its sources, be conceived as a process of causation; from the point of view of its issuance into a pattern of enjoyment, it may be conceived as a process of self-creation. Anticipation is a basic ingredient

----

[22]*Ibid.*, pp. 219-220. Used by permission.

in the process: one aims at realizing some ideal, perhaps in the immediate future, and this aim effectively conditions the present experience.

It is important to see that in his interpretation of nature Whitehead begins with concrete human experience. Thereby he enables us to see that the formulae of physics and chemistry represent a kind of one-eyed version of natural fact—reliable enough but deficient in depth, for the immediate facts of experience disclose nothing of a dead, feelingless, purposeless world, but quite the contrary. We can generalize from these facts to the whole of nature on the principle that they are on the same level as all other facts, though distinguished by their unusual complexity. One such distinguishing feature of our experience is consciousness. When Whitehead says we cannot understand nature apart from life, he does not mean that we must conceive nature as inherently conscious. Indeed, consciousness is a rare ingredient in life—life being essentially "the enjoyment of emotion, derived from the past and aimed at the future."[23] An occasion of life is in essence a creative activity whereby the welter of emotions supplied by antecedent occasions is brought into a unified pattern of emotion. We are unable to detect any flashes of consciousness at the "inorganic" level. The rudiments of consciousness are found above this level as "the faint direction of emphasis by unconscious ideal aim."[24] Among the higher mammals, especially in man, there is clear evidence that some degree of consciousness is ordinarily present.

We now have some inkling of Whitehead's vision of nature as alive and of the evidence on which it rests. Whitehead's two great interests—science and the humanities—converge in that vision. It is a vision which has power to liberate us from the materialism of the older science and put flesh on the abstract bones of the new.

[23] *Ibid.*, p. 229.
[24] *Ibid.*, p. 230.

CHAPTER IV

The Philosophy of Organism:

ITS UNDERPINNING

> *Any doctrine which refuses to place human experience outside nature, must find in descriptions of human experience factors which also enter into the descriptions of less specialized natural occurrences. If there be no such factors, then the doctrine of human experience as a fact within nature is mere bluff, founded upon vague phrases whose sole merit is a comforting familiarity. We should either admit dualism, at least as a provisional doctrine, or we should point out the identical elements connecting human experience with physical science.*
>
> Alfred North Whitehead[1]

No PHILOSOPHER can ply his craft without the tool of language. Learned during infancy and childhood, language carries insights from the past to each new generation. It also carries with it failures of insight. "For example, single words, each with its dictionary meaning, and single sentences, each bounded by full stops, suggest the possibility of complete abstraction from any environment."[2] Here, built into the very structure of language, we have a significant failure of insight. No fact can be (fully) understood apart from its context.

Language developed in order to express the prominent facts of experience, particularly the perceptions of the sense organs. "These prominent facts are the variable facts,—the appearance

---

[1]From *Adventures of Ideas*, p. 237. Reprinted with permission.
[2]Whitehead, *Modes of Thought*, p. 90.

of a tiger, of a clap of thunder, or of a spasm of pain."[3] But such facts, however vivid or important they may be, fail to disclose the underlying elements in experience. Only in intuitive flashes do we ever grasp these elements, and even then our language may be inadequate to express what we apprehend. The philosopher—who tries to verbalize his glimpses of the underlying elements—feels painfully cramped by the shortcomings of everyday language. "Words and phrases must be stretched towards a generality foreign to their ordinary usage."[4] In order to achieve greater adequacy of expression, Whitehead chooses at points to "redesign language." We can therefore expect from him a variety of terms and phrases which on first hearing sound strange to our ears.

Indeed, he employs a highly technical vocabulary in elaborating his theory of reality.[5] This vocabulary, he explains, was not pulled from a hat; it grew out of the writings of those great masters who laid the foundations of the theory. He has in mind (among others) the Englishman, F. H. Bradley (1846-1924), and the American, William James (1842-1910). Both men regarded feeling as the primary form of experience.[6]

To illustrate the way his technical vocabulary is grounded in a philosophical tradition, Whitehead cites the following statement from Bradley: "In my general feeling at any moment there is more than the objects before me, and no perception of objects will exhaust the sense of a living emotion."[7] Notice that for Bradley a feeling involves (1) objects, (2) living emotion, and (3) me, the one who feels. In general, Whitehead agrees with Bradley; but he prefers a somewhat different terminology. A

---

[3] Whitehead, *Adventures of Ideas*, p. 209.

[4] Whitehead, *Process and Reality*, p. 6.

[5] We sketched the theory in Chapter Three.

[6] This theory is far older than Bradley and James, and its germ may be found in Plato.

[7] Francis H. Bradley, *Essays on Truth and Reality* (Oxford: Oxford University Press, 1914), p. 159.

feeling, he says, involves (1) data (Bradley's "objects"), (2) subjective form (Bradley's "living emotion"), and (3) the subject (Bradley's "me"). The second term here (subjective form) is quite unfamiliar, and the best way to get hold of it is to remember that its meaning is close to "living emotion." Whitehead remarks: "My reason for using the term 'subjective form' is that I stretch its meaning beyond 'emotion'. For example consciousness, if it be present, is an element in the subjective form."[8] There can be no doubt, however, that for Whitehead "subjective form" refers *primarily* to the emotional reaction of a subject to its data. "The basis of experience," he writes, "is emotional. Stated more generally, the basic fact is the rise of an affective tone originating from things whose relevance is given."[9] When I experience the shriek of a fire siren, I am aware of emotion surging up in me, *bearing within itself* the loud, piercing sound on which my mind rivets attention. The soul of the experience is emotion—characterized by certain auditory qualities.

The word "feeling" not only implies emotion but also the apprehension of an object (or objects). One feels something or other or, as Whitehead puts it, one prehends something or other. His adoption of the term "prehension" (which literally means a seizing or grasping) illustrates again that his terminology has grown out of the writings of the great masters in his philosophical tradition. The German philosopher Leibniz (1646-1716) held that the world is composed of experiencing entities or, as he called them, "monads." He held that one monad can take account of another by "perception" (the lower way) or by "apperception" (the higher way). Whitehead employs neither term,[10] but he agrees that "all final individual actualities have

---

[8]Whitehead, *Adventures of Ideas*, p. 297.

[9]*Ibid.*, p. 226. Consciousness is not present in all experience; indeed, it appears only at the highest levels of experience.

[10]He says that "perception" and "apperception" both suggest consciousness as well as the theory that a subject directly experiences only images or ideas.

the metaphysical character of occasions of experience."[11] And in the style of Leibniz, he uses the label "prehension" for "the general way in which the occasion of experience can include, as part of its own essence, any other entity, whether another occasion of experience or an entity of another type."[12]

It may at first seem strange to say that the world is made up of occasions. But is there a better way to conceive and convey the dynamic, creative, living character of reality? A person's life certainly consists of a procession of events or occasions. Each occasion is linked to those that have come before it. Indeed, it is born out of the womb of the past. Although a newborn occasion bears its heritage within itself, it is—like any offspring—a fresh, new creation by virtue of its unique response to that heritage. It appropriates the occasions constituting its antecedent world, welding them into a unity according to its own purpose. Thus, past occasions are fused into the present occasion, which in turn becomes a datum for occasions yet unborn.

In a newborn occasion, then, the many (antecedent data) become one. Unification of things is not possible in any other way; nor can things even *be* except as elements of occasions of experience.[13] When we speak of data or objects provided by the past for unification in a present occasion, our words carry the misleading suggestion that the present occasion arises out of a purely passive state of affairs. The truth is that each of these data actively *compels* its embodiment, its reenaction, in the burgeoning occasion. It thrusts itself into the formation of the future and thereby acquires immortality. A datum in the antecedent world of a newborn occasion is simply an occasion that has completed its self-formation and perished in its hot, living immediacy. In perishing, it assumes a role in other-

---

[11]Whitehead, *Adventures of Ideas*, p. 284.

[12]*Ibid.*, p. 300.

[13]This is a basic principle in Whitehead's metaphysics. He calls it the "ontological principle."

formation, that is, in the birth of other (future) occasions.[14]

The past data from which a new occasion emerges constitute the "actual world" or "initial phase" of that occasion. Since these data as a whole are characterized by the urge toward the formation of new occasions, they can also be called a "real potentiality." "It belongs to the nature of a 'being,' " says Whitehead, "that it is a potential for every [subsequent] 'becoming.' "[15] The way past occasions propel themselves into the future and thereby provide the objects required for the formation of new occasions is termed "creativity." "The creativity of the world is the throbbing emotion of the past hurling itself into a new transcendent fact."[16] It is the ultimate metaphysical principle, in accord with which the world is ever achieving new instances of concrete unity (that is, "concrescences").

An occasion is not some sort of fully definite, enduring thing that *has* prehensions. *It is the outcome of its prehensions.* "For Kant, the world emerges from the subject; for the philosophy of organism [Whitehead's own philosophy], the subject emerges from the world."[17] The fact that the subject (or occasion) emerges from the world, that it creates itself by synthesizing past data according to its particular aim, suggests that an occasion is to be conceived as an organism—a term Whitehead uses as a label for his philosophy as a whole. The doctrine that an occasion is self-creating may seem unintelligible. The underlying issue is whether an occasion represents something really new under the sun. Whitehead's position is that with each

---

[14]Whitehead comments: "Almost all of *Process and Reality* can be read as an attempt to analyse perishing on the same level as Aristotle's analysis of becoming. The notion of the prehension of the past means that the past is an element which perishes and thereby remains an element in the state beyond, and thus is objectified. That is the whole notion. If you get a general notion of what is meant by perishing, you will have accomplished an apprehension of what you mean by memory and causality, what you mean when you feel that what we are is of infinite importance, because as we perish we are immortal. That is the one key thought around which the whole development of *Process and Reality* is woven." Whitehead, *Science and Philosophy*, pp. 125-126. Used by permission.

[15]Whitehead, *Process and Reality*, p. 33. This is Whitehead's "principle of relativity." It is simply a rendering of the ontological principle from the point of view of the relation of things to the future.

[16]Whitehead, *Adventures of Ideas*, p. 227.

[17]Whitehead, *Process and Reality*, pp. 135-136.

occasion there is "creative advance into novelty."[18] "The alternative to this doctrine," he observes, "is a static morphological universe."[19] Accordingly, he tries to give an account of a subject's emergence from the world.[20] While an occasion is a synthesis of past data (a notion neatly expressed by the term "concrescence"), it is more. For the "living emotion" that wells up within a concrescence constitutes an element of sheer novelty. An occasion achieves full-blown individuality at the moment its concrescence culminates in a unity of feeling (or subjective form). "The occasion arises from relevant objects, and perishes into the status of an object for other occasions. But it enjoys its decisive moment of absolute self-attainment as emotional unity."[21] In that moment the world has passed from the objectivity of the data to the subjectivity of the fully-developed occasion.

It is evident that Whitehead makes room for both the discrete and the continuous, both the pearls and the string. In the moment of self-completion, an occasion stands alone, an emotional unity existing in and for itself. Yet, it is a fruit of the past, and as such it embodies subjective forms belonging to its antecedent world (as occasions which succeed it will embody *its* subjective forms). Discreteness and continuity are important concepts in modern physics: there are the distinguishable individual facts— electrons, protons, photons, etc.—each a locus of energy; and there is the flow of energy in paths through time and space. But physics fails to tell the whole story of concrete process. The notion of physical energy, which is basic in physics, must "be conceived as an abstraction from the complex energy, emotional and purposeful, inherent in the subjective form of the final synthesis in which each occasion completes itself."[22]

---

[18]*Ibid.*, p. 529.

[19]*Ibid.*, p. 340.

[20]Actually, it would be more accurate to speak of a "superject" than of a "subject," since "the feelings [of an occasion] aim at the feeler, as their final cause." *Ibid.*, p. 339.

[21]Whitehead, *Adventures of Ideas*, p. 227.

[22]*Ibid.*, p. 239.

Since an occasion inherits subjective forms belonging to its antecedent world, we may regard that antecedent world as the occasion's cause. From another point of view, however, its cause is its own aim at a particular, unified way of feeling its data. Thus, an occasion emerging into actuality has two kinds of relation, one backward, one forward: it prehends its actual world "sympathetically" and its aim "appetitively." Its initial feelings conform to those of its objects, but it seeks a way of enjoying those objects that is unique to itself. Accordingly, Whitehead says that on the one hand an occasion has a "physical pole" (with its "physical prehensions") and on the other a "mental pole" (with its "conceptual prehensions").[23] Physical prehensions secure sympathetic identification with the past, while conceptual prehensions secure ideal contrast with the past. The occasion selects its ideal as to what it will make of itself from an infinity of possibilities (or "eternal objects" as Whitehead calls them).[24] Such a selection involves "the exclusion of the boundless wealth of *alternative* potentiality, and the inclusion of that definite factor of novelty which constitutes the selected way of entertaining those data [from the occasion's past] in that process of unification."[25] The eternal objects which an occasion includes not only express *how* past occasions enter into that occasion but also *how* each of its phases enters into the next until at last the unity it aims for is attained. Such attainment constitutes the occasion's final phase and is "termed the 'satisfaction,' since it marks the exhaustion of the creative urge for that individuality."[26] It also marks the living border of time beyond which lies the future. The occasion imposes upon the future the obligation of perpetuating it. Hence, in its final phase (and also earlier), it anticipates its own immortalization as an object in occasions yet to be. Thus, "the occasion arises as an effect facing its past and ends as a cause facing its future.

---

[23]The terms "mental" and "conceptual" do not in these usages imply consciousness.
[24]While the actual world of an occasion provides its "real potentiality," the eternal objects provide its "pure potentiality."
[25]Whitehead, *Modes of Thought*, pp. 207-208. Italics added.
[26]Whitehead, *Adventures of Ideas*, p. 248.

In between there lies the teleology [purposiveness] of the Universe."[27]

An occasion is much like a work of art, a painting, for instance. Beginning with canvas, brush, and paints, a painter brings about on the canvas a unity of colors and shapes, transforming the canvas stroke by stroke to suit his particular aim. The completed painting, with its unique aesthetic unity, is the outcome of the process. A completed occasion must also be viewed as an aesthetic unity—the outcome of its own concrescent process. In that process, the occasion omits none of the data belonging to its antecedent world.[28] But it can provide each of those data a niche in its completed, aesthetic unity only by adding elements of feeling by which to cement them all together. The process begins with public data capable of being cemented into unity, and ends in private enjoyment of those data so cemented. *How* an occasion feels its data depends on which eternal objects (possible patterns or structures) it admits into its concrescence.[29] The admission ("ingression") of eternal objects introduces freshness or newness, providing thereby a contrast with the old, that is, with given data. There may also be contrast among the eternal objects admitted into the concrescence. In addition, there is the general contrast between actual fact and unactualized eternal objects (possibilities): as candidates for actualization in an occasion, eternal objects furnish a sense of what may be, a "lure for feeling" as Whitehead puts it;[30] those rejected by the occasion haunt it with a sense of what might have been. These contrasts, built into the unity of the occasion, furnish the basis for its aesthetic character—in accordance with the principle that "all æsthetic experience is feeling arising out of the realization of contrast under identity."[31]

---

[27]*Ibid.*, p. 249.

[28]Various elements in the constitutions of occasions composing that antecedent world will be incompatible with one another, and some of these elements will therefore have to be relegated to irrelevance.

[29]Accordingly, eternal objects are called "forms of definiteness."

[30]See Whitehead, *Process and Reality*, p. 131.

[31]Whitehead, *Religion in the Making* (New York: The Macmillan Company, 1926), p. 115.

Perhaps a few words about the nature of eternal objects are in order. Whitehead's doctrine of eternal objects has an ancestry that goes back at least to Plato, who held that to a term such as "man" corresponds an independently existing form, *Man*. He regarded forms as supremely real, completely changeless, and fully self-sustaining.[32] From Whitehead's point of view, there's the rub. For a Platonic form violates the principle that "it belongs to the nature of a 'being' that it is a potential for every [subsequent] 'becoming.' "[33] Whitehead expresses his view of the matter as follows:

It is mere phantasy to impute to them [the forms] any 'absolute reality', which is devoid of implications beyond itself. The realm of forms is the realm of potentiality, and the very notion of 'potentiality' has an external meaning. It refers to life and motion. It refers to inclusion and exclusion. It refers to hope, fear, and intention. Phrasing this statement more generally,—it refers to appetition. It refers to the development of actuality, which realizes form and is yet more than form. It refers to past, present and future.[34]

Correlative with Plato's doctrine of the forms is his view of the temporal world as shadowy and relatively unreal. By contrast, Whitehead's position is that temporal process *is* reality and that forms (that is, eternal objects) are essentially relative to temporal process. His stand is reminiscent of Aristotle, who maintained that (on earth) forms are always embedded in matter. Indeed, Whitehead insists not only that eternal objects are relative to temporal process but in addition that they are resident in actuality even as sheer possibilities and are never "free-floating." They are, he holds, in the mind of God. "By this recognition of the divine element the general Aristotelian principle is maintained that, apart from things that are actual,

---

[32]Whitehead writes: "Plato in the earlier period of his thought, deceived by the beauty of mathematics intelligible in unchanging perfection, conceived of a super-world of ideas, forever perfect and forever interwoven. In his latest phase he sometimes repudiates the notion, though he never consistently banishes it from his thought." Whitehead, *Adventures of Ideas*, p. 354. Reprinted with permission.

[33]Whitehead, *Process and Reality*, p. 33.

[34]Whitehead, *Modes of Thought*, p. 95. Used by permission.

there is nothing."[35] We shall return to Whitehead's doctrine of God in the next chapter.

An eternal object characterizing one or more occasions will be reproduced in subsequent occasions as they each prehend it. The total group of occasions each of which thereby exhibits that eternal object is a "society" and the eternal object is its "defining characteristic." A society may consist of a single strand of occasions, one immediately following the next (up to the latest occasion). Such a society Whitehead calls a "person," the serial succession of its occasions being termed "personal order." A nonpersonal society is one involving occasions that are contemporary with one another, each of which, thanks to its prehension of antecedent members of the society, inherits the same eternal object. An ordinary physical object, a chair for example, is a nonpersonal society. So, too, are animal and vegetable bodies. "But most of the animals, including all the vertebrates, seem to have their social system [or society] dominated by a subordinate society which is 'personal'."[36] This is preeminently true of man.

Whereas an occasion simply comes into being and perishes, a society has the peculiar quality of enduring, that is, of continuing in its basic self-identity as a society. "A society has an essential character, whereby it is the society that it is, and it has also accidental qualities which vary as circumstances alter."[37] This statement, with its reference to changing circumstances, reminds us that every society has an environment. "In reference to any given society," Whitehead points out, "the world of actual entities [occasions] is to be conceived as forming a background in layers of social order, the defining characteristics becoming wider and more general as we widen the background."[38]

---

[35]Whitehead, *Process and Reality*, p. 64.
[36]Whitehead, *Adventures of Ideas*, p. 264.
[37]*Ibid.*, p. 262.
[38]Whitehead, *Process and Reality*, p. 138.

In this chapter we have taken a look at the underpinning of Whitehead's system. Our account has had the limited objective of putting before the reader certain key concepts of that system —a system whose exposition in a full and adequate way requires volumes. It is important to remember as one struggles to comprehend Whitehead that his writings represent an attempt to put in precise and technical language his vision of the world as living, feeling, growing. A vision into depths has been given expression.

CHAPTER V

The Philosophy of Organism:

ITS KEYSTONE

> *God's rôle is not the combat of productive force with productive force, of destructive force with destructive force; it lies in the patient operation of the overpowering rationality of his concepual harmonization. He does not create the world, he saves it: or, more accurately, he is the poet of the world, with tender patience leading it by his vision of truth, beauty, and goodness.*
> Alfred North Whitehead[1]

WHITEHEAD'S DOCTRINE of God is not a mere addition to his system, a kind of ornament or curlicue; on the contrary, it is central to his system, the keystone in the arch. Moreover, since we are concerned in this book with process philosophy as a framework for theological reflection, it is both important and appropriate to take a studied look at Whitehead's doctrine of God. I will content myself with stating its main elements, considering in turn God as primordial, as consequent, and as superjective (to use Whitehead's terminology). You see, Whitehead presents three aspects of the divine being, and his threefold presentation will furnish the topics for this chapter.

A consideration of the nature and status of possibilities will help us grasp Whitehead's concept of God as primordial. Possibilities are unseen realities that temper and guide our lives. Both

---

[1]*Ibid.*, pp. 525-526. Used by permission.

thankfulness and regret depend on one's ability to envisage possibilities, to envisage what *might* have been. Hope and fear also depend on one's ability to envisage possibilities, in this case, to envisage what *may* be. For Whitehead, any occasion of experience—whatever its place in the scale of nature—is in touch with the eternal objects or possibilities, from which it selects[2] a goal regarding its own self-fulfillment.

How are we to think of these eternal objects? Do they float like angels in the clouds? Whitehead's position is that they are resident in the mind of God. After all, when we speak of the possible, we are referring to the incomplete, unfinished aspect of something already in existence, to its capacity to add to itself new qualities. For example, almost any small child is able (in time) to add a cubit to his stature—as parents will be quick to acknowledge. The child, who is unquestionably "something already in existence," has before him the unfinished business of growing taller, that is, of further actualization; and such unfinished business on the part of an existing thing is just what we mean by possibility. But why must we—with Whitehead—conceive possibilities as ultimately attaching to God? Are not ordinary beings sufficient to provide a ground for possibility? In answering such questions, there is one decisive consideration: ordinary beings are always actualizations, selections from preexisting possibilities. In short, ordinary beings are contingent; they need not have existed at all, and something else might have been in their place. But if possibility is prerequisite to actualization and yet is to be conceived as the incomplete, unfinished aspect of some existing thing, *then not all existence is contingent.* Perhaps someone will grant that an ordinary being represents an actualization of preexisting possibilities, resident in something already in existence, but argue that the "something already in existence" is in every case merely a prior ordinary being (or prior ordinary beings) so that what we really have is an infinite

---

[2]Its selection, as we will see below, is always qualified by God's intention for it.

series of actualizations, each new ordinary being emerging out of possibilities attaching to past ordinary beings. However, a series of actualizations stretching back as far as one pleases represents *(as such)* a selection from possibility: precisely that series, if actual, must have been one of the possibilities. Possibility must then in the final analysis be the "unfinished business" of a being whose existence is not itself an actualization of possibility but rather an eternal fact, a being whose nonexistence is impossible —namely, God.

According to Whitehead, God does not stare frigidly at the eternal objects; he feels them appetitively, that is, with desire for future realization.

We must conceive the Divine Eros [that is, God as the ground of the eternal objects] as the active entertainment of all ideals, with the urge to their finite realization, each in its due season. Thus a process must be inherent in God's nature, whereby his infinity is acquiring realization.[3]

Indeed, it is precisely because of God's "active entertainment of all ideals, with the urge to their finite realization"—or in other words, because of his subjective aim—that an order is imposed on those ideals (eternal objects). For each gets its relation to all the others in accordance with the strength of God's desire for its realization. Thus, God establishes among the eternal objects an order of relevance to the creative advance of the world. He is then the fundamental and indispensable agent of that advance, regulating its course by his grading of the entire range of possibilities. While another regulation would have been possible, none would have been superior.

Each occasion feels God's urge toward realization of this or that possibility respecting its antecedent world; the occasion reproduces in its primary phase God's thrust toward those possibilities. In this way God provides the "germ" of the occasion's

---

[3]Whitehead, *Adventures of Ideas*, p. 357. Reprinted with permission.

aim at self-completion. Whitehead is here expressing the insight that God's own impulses inspire and guide the creatures. He is saying that each creature at the core of its being has an immediate, sympathetic awareness (in short, a love) of God by virtue of which God's own yearnings are transmitted to it. As the ultimate impulse behind each instance of concrete reality, God is in Whiteheadian terms the "principle of concretion" (or of limitation). It was just this—that God is the ultimate impulse behind each occasion—that Whitehead had in mind when, in the quotation at the head of the chapter, he said that God does not create the world. He inspires it by his vision of truth, beauty, and goodness, and only in this sense can he be said to create it.

The fact that God determines the general course of things does not mean that he determines everything. An occasion "derives from God its basic conceptual aim, relevant to its actual world, *yet with indeterminations awaiting its own decisions.*"[4] In other words, God is not the only being who makes decisions (who selects among possibilities). Each occasion is *partly* self-determining—even though it derives its basic aim from God. To use Whitehead's phrase, the occasion is a "self-creating creature."[5] Its decisions have to do with the completion of what God has initiated, namely, its own concrete selfhood. In a local and secondary sense, then, the occasion is also a "principle of concretion," determining by sheer fiat the details of its fruition as a fully concrete fact. The freedom of individual occasions requires some kind of overall coordination of each occasion with all the others, for without such coordination the occasions would simply frustrate and checkmate one another, and the result would be chaos. If it is unlikely that a committee could have painted the *Mona Lisa,* it is all the more unlikely that the multiplicity of occasions could have produced cosmic order. They lack the wisdom and power to do so. What is required

---

[4]Whitehead, *Process and Reality,* p. 343. Italics added.
[5]*Ibid.,* p. 130.

is a cosmic individual who by his all-pervasive influence gives shape and direction to things. The fact that the world requires a single source of order brings us again to the doctrine of God as the ground of the eternal objects, for, as we have seen, the requisite coordination of things is brought about by virtue of the fact that each occasion is swayed by God's own ideals. He exercises his providential influence over the world not by push and pull, but by persuasion. There is nothing farfetched about this. Everyone knows that a lover is captivated by the charms of the one he loves, that a man is inspired by the faith and appreciation of his colleagues, that a student is guided by the expectations of his teachers, that a youth is influenced by the hopes and wishes of his parents, and that an artist is controlled by his vision of beauty. So, too, the occasions of the world are lured and in this sense controlled by the power of God's ideals.

God's persuasive control over the world is not unlike a man's control over his own body. Suppose, for example, that the man wishes to speak to a friend. In order to do so, he does not manipulate his lungs, vocal cords, tongue, lips, etc., in the way a locomotive pushes and pulls cars about on a track. Rather, his thoughts, feelings, and desires *inspire* his body into the production of speech. He controls by persuading. The power of this analogy for theological thought has yet to be fully explored.

God's envisagement of the eternal objects is presupposed by every actualization; it is, as Whitehead says, "primordial." God's primordial experience is beyond imagination, composed as it is of purely conceptual feelings, that is, feelings in commerce with the possibilities-for-all-possible-worlds, but in commerce with no actualities. Using familiar theological terminology, we can say that God's envisagement of the eternal objects is his will or purpose. However, since "will" or "purpose" suggests consciousness, this is somewhat misleading. For not only do purely conceptual feelings lack fullness of actuality, they also lack consciousness (which arises only in cases where physical

71

and are not."[7] A man who is planning to build a house may waver among various styles of architecture, but he knows that the house he builds will have some particular style or other, that it cannot have all possible styles and still be one house. Since the principle that not all possibilities are compatible applies to the possibilities for good, "there is no totality which is the harmony of all perfections."[8] God cannot therefore be the *actual* realization of all possible goodness, though he is the *conceptual* realization of all possible goodness—as of every possibility. Whitehead describes the divine conceptual realization as "free, complete, primordial, eternal, actually deficient, and unconscious."[9]

To identify God with his conceptual experience would be to commit the Fallacy of Misplaced Concreteness, for as conceptual, God is without consciousness, without achievement, and without fullness of actuality or relation. His conceptual side can no more be separated from his concrete fullness than the grin of the Cheshire cat can be separated from the cat. Above we remarked that Whitehead speaks of this concrete fullness as "consequent." The term suggests that God's actual experience arises by virtue of his receptivity to the occasions making up the world. It may, therefore, be said that "God's persuasion of us is balanced by our persuasion of him."[10] The consequent side of God's life "originates with physical experience derived from the temporal world, and then acquires integration with the primordial side. It is determined, incomplete, consequent, 'everlasting,' fully actual, and conscious."[11] To say that God as consequent (dependent) on the world is incomplete implies that every future actualization will add content to his experience. Since the wealth of possibility is boundless, it is

---

[7] Whitehead, *Adventures of Ideas*, p. 356.
[8] *Ibid.*
[9] Whitehead, *Process and Reality*, p. 524.
[10] Hartshorne, "Whitehead's Idea of God," *The Philosophy of Alfred North Whitehead*, ed. Paul Arthur Schilpp (New York: Tudor Publishing Company, 1951), p. 553.
[11] Whitehead, *Process and Reality*, p. 524. Used by permission.

inexhaustible. Consequently, any and all actualization, including God's, must be finite—always less than what is possible. An actuality, however, is a unit of realized value and as such is superior to the entire multiplicity of eternal objects. In his consequent experience God includes all the actualities of the infinite past, right down to the present. Accordingly, his consequent experience is always richer than that of any other being—or of all other beings—and is always richer than his own experience at any previous time. *In this sense,* God as consequent is complete and unsurpassable.

Whitehead is referring to God's retention of the actualities of the infinite past when he describes God's consequent experience as "everlasting." It is an empirical fact, Whitehead observes, that temporal process involves loss. Time marches on—and takes with it even the most precious of possessions. We look back nostalgically to "the glory that was Greece" or treasure memories of a departed loved one or wistfully recall the delicious irresponsibility of childhood. Once upon a time . . . but no longer. Can this be the whole story—the last word? Whitehead writes: "Just as physical feelings are haunted by the vague insistence of causality, so the higher intellectual feelings are haunted by the vague insistence of another order, where there is no unrest, no travel, no shipwreck: 'There shall be no more sea.' "[12]

Why is there loss in the temporal process? The reason is simply that in the antecedent world of an occasion there are mutually obstructive factors. In order to achieve its unity, the occasion must attenuate (play down) some of these factors, at times reducing them to zero intensity, that is, to irrelevance. However, God has a resource no creature possesses, namely, his all-inclusive grasp of possibilities.[13] In receiving the world's

[12]*Ibid.,* p. 516. Used by permission.
[13]Whitehead writes: "The perfection of God's subjective aim, derived from the completeness of his primordial nature, issues into the character of his consequent nature. In it [the consequent nature] there is no loss, no obstruction." *Ibid.,* p. 524.

actualities, therefore, he is not at the mercy of mutually obstructive factors, forced to select among them and hence discard some elements in the actual world. As Whitehead puts it,
he employs "intermediate elements"[14] among the discordant
factors to bring about their adjustment into a complex unity.
God, then, is able to bring the infinity of occasions into harmonious unity, retaining them all without loss or obstruction.
He has the wisdom and patience to do what no creature can
do, namely, to preserve all occasions in the ongoing unity of
his life, of which every new occasion is destined to become a
constitutive part. As Whitehead said in the quotation at the
opening of the chapter, God saves the world. "The wisdom of
[God's] subjective aim prehends every actuality for what it can
be in such a perfected system—its sufferings, its sorrows, its
failures, its triumphs, its immediacies of joy—woven by right-
ness of feeling into the harmony of the universal feeling, which
is always immediate, always many, always one, always with
novel advance, moving onward and never perishing."[15]

Whitehead speaks of God as "superjective" as well as primordial and consequent. He means that the world feels (prehends) God's reception of it into his own experience, that is, it
feels God as consequent. An occasion does not feel God's reception of itself, but it does feel the objects in its antecedent
actual world as elements in his consequent experience. Hence,
each occasion in a personally ordered society (that is, an enduring personality) feels the past members of that society as
parts of the divine life. Accordingly, an occasion is always
aware, if only vaguely, of God's saving love for the world—of
his "particular providence for particular occasions."[16] An occasion finds refreshment in the sense that it will occupy in God's
experience the most appropriate place of which it is capable
and will live there forevermore in unfading importance.

---

[14]*Ibid.*, p. 517.
[15]*Ibid.*, p. 525. Used by permission.
[16]*Ibid.*, p. 532.

CHAPTER VI

A New Advocate

> *It is my belief that our age has the privilege of producing a*
> *neglected alternative both to the old speculative theology or*
> *metaphysics, and to the mere rejection of all metaphysics*
> *and theology, an alternative as significantly new as rela-*
> *tivity physics or quantum mechanics, yet attractive not sim-*
> *ply in that it is new, but because it renders substantial*
> *justice to both parties in many an old battle. In other words,*
> *there is a novel "higher synthesis" which offers promise of*
> *being not merely one more doctrine to fight over, but, to some*
> *extent at least, a transcending of the causes of conflict. Many*
> *men have been creating this synthesis, and most of all, the late*
> *A. N. Whitehead. My own lesser degree of inventiveness is for*
> *others to assess, if they care to.*
>
> Charles Hartshorne[1]

WHEN WHITEHEAD RETIRED from teaching at Harvard in 1937, he was seventy-six, and his lifework was near completion. In the decade which remained to him, he published his last book, *Modes of Thought,* and in addition some eight articles. Then, on December 30, 1947, he was gone. Over the years his ideas had taken root in students, colleagues, and readers, some of whom have since become eminent as exponents of his philosophy. Charles Hartshorne[2] is one of these, and in this chapter we will

---

[1]From *Reality as Social Process,* p. 18. Used by permission.

[2]Hartshorne was born the son of an Episcopal clergyman in the town of Kittanning, Pennsylvania, on June 5, 1897. His college career, begun at Haverford in 1915, was interrupted by World War I, and he spent the years 1917-19 as an orderly in an army hospital in France. After the war, he went to Harvard. Here he earned three degrees, including the doctorate. From 1923 to 1925 he studied in Germany, as a Sheldon Fellow, at Freiburg and Marburg. In 1925 he became an instructor and later a research fellow in philosophy at Harvard, working continuously on the manuscripts of C. S. Peirce. During one semester he served as assistant to Whitehead. He continued at Harvard until 1928, when he joined the faculty of the University of Chicago. (We can be sure that during the three years 1925-28, when Hartshorne was associated with Whitehead at Harvard, he soaked up much of Whitehead's philosophy.) He was at Chicago twenty-seven years. In addition, he was visiting professor at Stanford, the New School for Social Research, Goethe University in Frankfurt, Germany, and Melbourne University, Australia (Fulbright). During his last twelve years at Chicago, he was a member of the theological faculty as well as of the philosophy department. In 1955 he became professor of philosophy at Emory University in Atlanta. In 1958 Hartshorne was visiting professor at the University of Washington and then Fulbright Professor at Kyoto University, Japan. He joined the department of philosophy at the University of Texas in 1962, being appointed Ashbel Smith Professor in 1963.

take a look at some of his emphases. It will become evident as we proceed that Hartshorne agrees substantially with Whitehead. Hartshorne is no carbon copy of Whitehead,[3] but plainly he uses and develops the main themes of Whiteheadian philosophy. Because he has devoted much of his life to the development of the doctrine of God within and beyond the context of Whitehead's metaphysics, Hartshorne is of special interest to Christian theologians.

One who sits in Hartshorne's classroom has the impression he is viewing the interior workings of a mind. Hartshorne, even when he speaks the whole hour, does not so much lecture as carry on a dialogue with himself, a dialogue he is prepared to interrupt whenever students have questions or comments. Under his auspices philosophy is never a cut and dried affair, a numbing digest of this opinion and that. He is forever in the thick of battle, and a student is easily caught up in the excitement of it. Seated at the desk in front of his class, he will peer at the blackboard or out the window as he talks. At times one finds him preoccupied with thoughts that consume his full attention. Aside from philosophy, he has made the study of birdsong his hobby and has to his credit ten or more articles in journals of ornithology.

What are some of the planks in Hartshorne's philosophical platform? There are three which are fundamental, and all of them reveal the close tie between Hartshorne and Whitehead. In the first place, there is Hartshorne's doctrine that at base everything is psychic, a doctrine for which he uses the label "panpsychism" (from the Greek for "all" and "soul"). Hartshorne presents it thus: "The insentient, dead, and mechanical is secondary to, or even a mere appearance or special case of, the sentient, living, and social."[4] He is not suggesting that the underlying psychic reality is to be conceived in terms of *our*

---

[3]Hartshorne had expounded panpsychism in his doctoral thesis before he had even heard of Whitehead.

[4]Hartshorne, *Reality as Social Process*, pp. 132-133.

form of experience—though there is assuredly a kinship between the human and nonhuman types. Indeed, Hartshorne says
we need an interpretation of "experience" (and related notions)
that will apply all up and down the line.[5] We have seen that
Whitehead attempts just such an interpretation.

I suppose most people would grant that at least the higher
animals are (in Hartshorne's words) "sentient, living, and
social." But what of the lower animals, what of plants, and
especially what of that vast domain we are accustomed to call
"inorganic"? As for the lower animals, Hartshorne argues that
the same principle applies to them as to the higher animals,
namely, that physiology is the clue to psychology. Thus, to the
extent that an animal, whether higher or lower, differs from
us in physiological make-up, we may suppose that it also differs
from us in psychological make-up, *but not that it lacks psychological aspects altogether.* The fact that an animal has
no nerves is not proof that it is unable to feel, any more than
the fact that an animal has no muscles is proof that it is unable
to move. As for plants, Hartshorne points out that they differ
from animals chiefly in their mode of organization. For both
plants and animals are cellular, and the distinction between
vegetable and animal life is of little importance when we com-
pare single cells with one another.[6] By and large, multicellular
animals are integrated wholes, whereas multicellular plants are
simply colonies of cells. The movement of a plant toward light
is actually the movement of a crowd whose members individually move toward the light. In contrast to plants, animals
appear to possess sensation, feeling, and memory. But while a
plant itself is merely a nonsentient group, its constituent cells
may very well be sentient individuals. Much the same can be
said of "inorganic" objects. For such an object, though it cannot plausibly be regarded as something living or sentient, may
consist of living, sentient parts—whether molecular, atomic, or

[5]See Hartshorne, "Present Prospects for Metaphysics," *The Monist*, Vol.
47 (Winter, 1963), 197.
[6]Cf. *ibid.*

subatomic. If response to environmental conditions and unity of action are basic marks of experience, a stone or piece of metal is surely bereft of experience. "But when we come to individual molecules, atoms, or electrons, the lack of dynamic integrity characteristic of many larger objects can no longer be so confidently asserted."[7] Perhaps then "matter" is not another realm alongside "mind" or "experience"—Whitehead, we saw, emphatically denies that it is—but rather the appearance of a multitude of experient individuals when they are seen from the outside.

Hartshorne has no patience with the doctrine that a changeless something or other (called a "substance") underlies the qualities of an object—somewhat as a pincushion underlies the pins that are stuck in it. We may be prone to assume some such thing. For example, we may suppose that an apple is a substance possessing qualities such as redness, juiciness, roundness, etc. But on examination the "stuff" of everyday objects turns out to be a compound of parts, each of which is a compound of parts, each of which is in turn a compound of parts, and so on, until we finally arrive at the ultramicroscopic level where there are simply events related to one another in relatively permanent patterns. "Thus, events and their forms and relationships (such as similarity, causal influence, or memory), are all the 'substance' we can give any positive meaning to."[8] It is important to emphasize, however, that events compounded at any level may achieve genuine individuality at that level— depending on whether the society of events is sufficiently integrated to act as a unit. A society may consist of members all of which are of similar grade, or it may contain one radically superior member which unifies and directs the entire society. A man is a society of cells, each of which is a relatively low-grade individual, plus the human personality, a high-grade

[7] Hartshorne, *Reality as Social Process*, p. 133.
[8] Charles Hartshorne, *The Logic of Perfection* (La Salle, Illinois: The Open Court Publishing Company, 1962), p. 222.

individual, which integrates the whole. Clearly, Hartshorne's panpsychism continues a basic Whiteheadian thesis.

Hartshorne declares that panpsychism is false to nothing we know about the world. Of course, we may be unable to *discern* life within plants and minerals, but this fact must be interpreted with care. If my wife asks me whether our son's missing shoe is somewhere in the closet, I may look in the closet and report that I have not found it, but it would be rash to conclude that it is not there. The Greek philosopher, Aristotle, said that part of nature is inanimate, but this was not something he actually knew. What he knew was that he had failed to perceive individual agency, at least with respect to minerals. "But where we fail to perceive individuality of action this negative fact, this failure, must not be turned into a positive affirmation, a success, the insight that no such individuality is present in that part of nature."[9] The question is whether perception *should* be expected to disclose the nature of things at every possible level. If—as the German philosopher Leibniz believed —perception furnishes only a vague outline of physical objects, their constituents may very well be hidden from view and only indirectly accessible. In any event, " 'inanimateness' in the absolute sense never was or could be a fact; but it *seemed* to be so, by a natural illusion of commonsense and primitive science."[10]

Evidently, Hartshorne does not propose to rely exclusively upon the senses to tell him about nature. But if not, can he suggest some other way by which nature can be known, a way that would enable us to detect the feelings or experiences of its individual members? He admits that we do not directly share the experiences of other human beings, except in the most limited way. However, we do *infer* their experiences—and even those of the higher animals. For, as Hartshorne suggests, the look on a man's face, the posture he assumes, and the be-

---

[9] Hartshorne, *The Monist*, Vol. 47, 201.
[10] *Ibid.*

havior he goes through all convey to an observer a sense of the emotions, sensations, etc., he is experiencing; and if the experiences of other men can thus be inferred, cannot those of nonhuman vertebrates, at least to some extent? On a recent visit to the Cleveland Zoo I noticed that the adults in our party were every bit as enthralled by the animals as were the children. They wondered whether the polar bears missed their native habitat, whether the rhino was hostile, whether the penguins liked to perform for the crowd. No one supposed that these creatures were without experience, and everyone had some inkling as to how they felt. Where in the scale of nature are we to locate the lower limit of experience? "Is it the lowest vertebrates, the amoeba, the virus 'cell,' radioactive molecule, or what?"[11]

If participation in the experiences of other human beings and in those of the higher animals is largely indirect and inferential, there are nonetheless two kinds of direct, nonsensuous participation in the experiences of others. (1) We feel the feelings of our own bodies, especially of our nerve cells. We may not be accustomed to the idea that our bodies are "others," but in fact they are portions of the external world and continuous with it. While I am intimately, directly, and sympathetically associated with my body, there is always a spatial contrast between myself *here* and my bodily experience *there*. "The pain which I feel in my finger is my pain. Yet I can have varying degrees of identification with the pain, can contrast it as content 'there' in the finger with myself as spectator 'here,' i.e., vaguely in the head and chest region."[12] (2) We share the feelings of our own past selves. Strictly speaking, we are not identical with those past selves, yet the bond with the past is so close that ordinarily we do not distinguish the self of the present from the selves of the past, particularly from the self of the immediate past. "Memory is direct verification of

[11]Hartshorne, *The Logic of Perfection*, p. 309.
[12]Hartshorne, *Philosophy of Science*, II, 298.

the hypothesis of different individuals with more or less similar feelings."[13] It is obvious that in this analysis of our relation to our bodies and to our past selves Hartshorne follows Whitehead closely.

We are now in a position to consider a second major feature of Hartshorne's system, namely, his creationist view of time. According to Hartshorne, an individual is *essentially social:* its relations make it what it is. We are, of course, familiar with the fact that in interpersonal relations, what someone thinks of us enters profoundly into our self-appraisal; indeed, the man who claims he does not care what anyone thinks of him is either fibbing or fooling himself. But in panpsychism the principle that the relations of an individual enter profoundly into his make-up is broadened and extended to individuals at any level whatsoever. If individual A experiences individual B, the relationship is *internal* to A, not merely additional to A. A is simply an-individual-related-to-B. Accordingly, with a different object we will have a (somewhat) different subject. The fact that an individual is constituted by its relations suggests that relativity (in this context) can be taken to mean "varying with the variable." Or, as Hartshorne spells it out, relation "is the ability of a thing to express in its own nature those other things which, among alternatively possible or contingent things, happen to exist."[14] Here too the similarity to Whitehead is quite obvious.

It should be noted that A's experience of B does not relativize (change or affect) B. For it is not true that every term of a relation must be constituted by that relation. B, the object of A's experience, is *externally* related to A's experiencing of it.[15] The main point is that a term of a relation need in no sense involve that relation. The relation is, of course, possessed by

---

[13]*Ibid.*

[14]Hartshorne, *The Divine Relativity* (New Haven: Yale University Press, 1948), p. 33.

[15]However, "an external relation is only *nominally* a relation 'of' the term to which it is external." *Ibid.*, p. 65. Italics added.

some term, and this term will possess whatever the relation possesses. Hence, it will include every other term of the relation. Hartshorne uses the following example. If Harry Truman knows something about George Washington, this knowledge-of-Washington genuinely describes Truman; it is internal to him. But Truman's knowing Washington is not part of the description of Washington; it is entirely external to him. Note that this example involves the relation of two noncontemporary individuals, the later being the subject of which the earlier is the object. It illustrates the principle that past and present are related asymmetrically (that is, in one direction only), for while the past is internal to the present, the present is always external to the past. Thus, the past is in truth nonrelative or absolute with respect to the present, the nonrelative or absolute being anything neutral or indifferent to relational alternatives. To be sure, an individual may anticipate (indeed, may even necessitate) being remembered or known by some future subject or other. But this does not imply that the individual would experience any future *actual* subjects (and thereby be relativized), for "some future subject or other" is merely a universal—a kind or type without concrete content.

The reader may have found all this a pretty strong dish of tea, especially for one gulp. But it is necessary to indulge in a few technicalities in order to grasp Hartshorne's doctrine of time. In accord with the above sketch of temporal relations, Hartshorne conceives time as cumulative. For while the present can have no relation to future particulars,[16] it can (and does) have relation to past particulars, and "what has relation to X has X, for X is a constituent of relation-to-X."[17] But if a past particular is a constituent of the present, does it cease to be past? It does not, Hartshorne explains, for the simple reason

---

[16]"Future particulars" would be actualities existing in advance of their actualization. To avoid this absurdity, we must say either that no particular is yet to be actualized (in short, that there *is* no future) or with Hartshorne that the present is related to no particulars belonging to the future, since the future as such lacks particularity.

[17]Hartshorne, *The Divine Relativity*, p. 69.

that part of a whole is never identical with that whole. A present actuality is a whole which is included by nothing. When a new and more inclusive whole possesses it as a part, it is "no longer present but past." Thus, the doctrine of internal and external relations, as applied to time, really has to do with the relationship of part and whole—and with the principle that part and whole may be (and in temporal process always are) related asymmetrically: "XY is not itself without X, but X may be itself without XY."[18] The French philosopher Bergson remarks that time is like a snowball which accumulates layer upon layer of snow as it rolls along. To use another analogy, time is like a tree, which adds a new ring to its trunk each year.

Every event, though it includes in itself past events, is a new totality. Time is continuous gain in richness of concrete content, for it involves "the actualization of new terms related, whose relata include old terms independent of the new relations."[19] Now, since the old terms do not include the new, actualization is to be conceived, as in Whitehead, as the incoming of genuine novelty. Hartshorne agrees with Bergson that time is creation— or nothing. It is not, however, creation *ex nihilo* (out of nothing), for every actualization occurs within a context of real possibilities, that is, within the bounds of what *can* occur here and now. It is thinkable—logically possible—for Socrates to have been the first man on the moon, but a Socratic lunar landing was not *really* possible. Real possibility is restriction placed upon logical possibility by the course of events down to and including the present. However, real possibility is never as complete and definite as actuality. If it were, what could the future add that is not already present in its real possibility? Any event, therefore, is caused in that it issues from restricted or real possibility; it is self-creating in that it decides its particularity, its full definiteness, within the bounds of what is

----

[18]*Ibid.*
[19]*Ibid.*, p. 112. Relata are the things between (or among) which relations obtain.

really possible for it. The real possibility of an event "is as innocent of the precise quality as it is of the actuality of the event in question, and indeed the precise or particular quality *is* the actuality."[20] It is a startling and wondrous fact, too often missed, that the present is the edge of creation, that each event emerges into actuality with the freshness and newness of the biblical dawn of creation.

Long ago Aristotle laid down the principle that one concrete thing cannot qualify (that is, be the property of) another. This *seems* obvious enough. We do not, for example, make Jim a property of John. But if, as Hartshorne and Whitehead insist, subjects are essentially relative to and inclusive of their objects, Aristotle's principle cannot be maintained. Nonetheless, Hartshorne grants that "our experience is extremely vague or faint in most of its intuitions of predicates, and hence of the individuals included in some of these."[21] If a concrete object is not effectively intuited, it will not be included in all its richness in the intuiting subject. This suggests that time may involve loss (not just gain) in definiteness, that at least some of the concrete past is contained in no experience whatsoever. Of course, on the panpsychic view, nature is composed from top to bottom of sentient individuals, each of which intrinsically refers to past actualities. But if human experience is "extremely vague or faint," can we believe that subhuman experience is entirely clear and distinct? And do not humans—and most likely all other creatures—forget more than they retain? Moreover, for us and doubtless for creatures of any type, most of the concrete past, extensive as it is, is simply unavailable in any genuine sense. But how are we to give an account of an event which is neither occurring now nor part of what is occurring now? Where in all of reality is such an event—or has it absolutely ceased to be? If events *can* somehow slip into utter nonbeing, is truth about events which have so "slipped" really possible?

---

[20]Hartshorne, *Reality as Social Process,* p. 98.
[21]Hartshorne, *The Divine Relativity,* p. 114.

Surely truth about absolutely nothing is indistinguishable from no truth at all. Yet, we readily assume that there is truth about events which are unknown (perhaps even unknowable) to us or to any creature. If this assumption is not baseless—if, that is, events are somehow imperishable—what is required is a superhuman subject whose relativity to those events is such as to include them without any loss whatsoever.

Here we have the germ of an argument for the existence of God. Thus, we have come upon a third major feature of Hartshorne's system, one that bulks large in his writings—his theism, which in its basic structure agrees with that of Whitehead.

Hartshorne conceives God as the supremely social—supremely relative—being. Hence, in contrast to the mainstream of classical Christian theology, he regards God as processive, each of his successive experiences depending upon and including what actually happens in the world. Yet, in accord with the mainstream of classical Christian theology, our philosopher holds that the character of God—his essence—is wholly changeless. Thus, on the one hand, Hartshorne's conception of God shares with pantheism the doctrine that God is all-inclusive, though it differs from pantheism in holding that God's character is independent of the world. On the other hand, his conception shares with classical theism the doctrine that the divine character is fixed or absolute, though it differs from classical theism in distinguishing God's character from his relative, concrete states of experience. In Hartshorne's doctrine, then, God is dipolar—both absolute and relative—and to this doctrine Hartshorne attaches the name "panentheism." In most respects his doctrine parallels that of Whitehead, but the Hartshornian divine dipolarity cannot be identified with the dipolarity of primordial and consequent natures.

When we speak of the character or essence of God (what makes God always himself), we are referring to those changeless but abstract features which belong to God no matter what his concrete experiences may be. Knowledge of God's character does

87

not open his concrete experience to us any more than the knowledge that my neighbor is an honest man gives me access to his present thoughts and feelings. God's character is within his states of experience much as the past is in the present, namely, as a nonrelative (absolute) part in a relative whole.[22] But if in addition to his changeless essence, which he includes as an abstract factor within his total being, God (being supremely relative) includes all past actualities as concrete constituents of his experience and is destined to include all future actualities, how can he be perfect?

This question immediately suggests a prior question: what do we mean by "perfect"? The word has been taken to mean "incapable of increase in value or reality." If God is perfect in this sense, he is self-identical (the selfsame being) no matter what occurs in the world. Hartshorne points out that one who so conceives divine perfection faces a dilemma, for the perfect being either does or does not include all the imperfect beings. If it does include them, "then it is inferior to a conceivable perfection whose constituents would be more perfect."[23] If the perfect being does not include them, then it plus the imperfect beings is a totality greater than the perfect being alone—unless one is willing to concede that imperfect beings have neither value nor reality. Thus, if one holds that the world has so much as a flicker of value or reality, he is obliged to grant that there can be no perfection in the sense under consideration.

Perhaps divine perfection can be defined in another way, for if God is all-inclusive, what other being could possibly rival him? It is (paradoxically) in virtue of his unexceptionable relativity that God is superior to any other being, actual or possible. Still, since God in any one of his states includes all his previous states—and more—he continuously surpasses himself. Accordingly, God may be conceived as perfect in the sense of "the self-

---

[22]Of course, a past event is relative to its predecessors, whereas the divine character is relative in no way.

God's states of experience, like all events, are relative only to past data.

[23]Hartshorne, *The Divine Relativity,* p. 19.

surpassing surpasser of all others." It is the *manner* or *character* of God's relativity (namely, its unique adequacy) that is strictly absolute, that is, invariant no matter how other things vary.

It is not only true that God is relative to the world; it is also true that every subject is relative to God, though in an imperfect way. This is entirely in accord with Whitehead's view. Thus, man is relative to God even though his relativity to God is radically deficient: "Though it is vastly less true to say that we do than that we do not 'have' or include God, both statements are true."[24] Divine relativity is unrestricted and literal, while nondivine relativity is limited and approximate. The same sort of contrast holds for any of the metaphysical categories. This points up the uniqueness of God and makes hash of the charge that panentheism simply attributes human characteristics to the Deity. God is the one and only individual whose identity can be defined in purely rational or philosophical terms—that is, by reference to the categories alone.[25]

Creaturely relativity, however, is not without importance. On the contrary, it is the means by which God orders the world, for God's aims and ideals are incorporated into the world through the experiences that the creatures have of God, and these aims and ideals furnish a "persuasion" (Whitehead) over the course of events which falls short of coercion. In the absence of such control, the world would lapse into a chaotic state wherein subjects would thwart and nullify one another. Hartshorne conjectures that in controlling the world God sets the limits of freedom in such a way that the most favorable relation between risk and opportunity is maintained.

It will occur to a student of Hartshorne's doctrine to inquire whether God in his all-inclusiveness shares the pain, ignorance, and moral evil present in the world. As to his sharing the world's pain, we may give a brief answer.[26] Pain cannot be defined ade-

---

[24]*Ibid.*, p. 92.

[25]He "is the *one individual conceivable a priori.*" *Ibid.*, p. 31.

[26]For a fuller treatment, see the following chapter.

quately as the absence of pleasure: it is essentially a positive quality, and God in experiencing the world's pain—its misery, sorrow, and misfortune—must himself suffer that pain. Hence, he suffers not only the wealth but the burden of the world. Note that Hartshorne in taking this stand sets aside the age-old theory that God is utterly incapable of suffering. In addition, he sets aside the age-old theory that God's happiness is to be conceived as an unincreasable fullness, as absolute bliss.

Is ignorance, too, a part of God? Hartshorne observes that a whole can never share all the properties of its parts, a part being distinguished from the whole (of which it is a part) precisely by its *lack* of wholeness, that is, by its partialness. In other words, the whole always lacks the lack of wholeness which is the property of its part. Likewise, God contains beings as his own parts without including their ignorance as his own. He knows all things precisely as they are and accordingly lacks the lack of wholeness—the partialness—that characterizes the knowledge possessed by those beings. In short, ignorance is a negative quality (a lack of knowledge), lack of which is surely no defect. Of course, God knows *that* creatures are ignorant, and even though he does not share their ignorance, he possesses whatever positive qualities attach to them *qua* ignorant.

According to Hartshorne, moral evil is a special form of ignorance, one that involves intentional heedlessness (lack of awareness) of another's interests and feelings. This does not mean that a man who is morally evil will not know what another's interests and feelings are. It means he will not share the other's weal and woe concretely but will by intention exclude such sharing. Callousness is impossible for God, since he feels the feelings of every creature. Callousness *is* lack of feeling—a deficiency that God necessarily lacks. He is, of course, aware of moral evil as a fact wherever it exists, and he possesses whatever is positive about it. It follows that the discord which accompanies moral evil is taken into his experience, for, as Hartshorne says, discord is not negative: it is the *positive presence* of elements that clash. Accordingly, God endures aesthetic evil. It is important to note Hartshorne's point that while aesthetic evil is *endured,* moral evil is *enacted.* The only evil that pertains to God in any sense is aesthetic evil, which arises, at least in part, as a result of free, creaturely enactments. Hence, while God suffers all things positive, he does not choose all things.

Both ignorance and moral evil, then, are essentially negative. They involve exclusion of some object or objects. But to argue that God, since he is all-inclusive, must share the exclusion involved in either ignorance or moral evil is to argue that a whole must share the exclusion or partialness of its parts. The fact that one part of a whole excludes another part cannot be taken to mean that the whole excludes that other part. God as the inclusive whole does not share the exclusions of the creatures, whether cognitive or moral, though he is aware that those exclusions exist and shares all their positive aspects.

Such, in brief, is Hartshorne's position. It is evident that we have in him a new and vigorous advocate of process philosophy. It would not be a mistake to regard him as Whitehead's successor. However, Hartshorne has not just borrowed his philosophy from the great master. He reports that even before he became acquainted with academic philosophy, he had arrived at the idea that all reality is psychic. In those early years he also came vaguely to believe that God is processive, a belief which he later found convincingly defended by his teacher W. E. Hocking.[27] Nonetheless, Hartshorne's philosophy is remarkably consonant with Whitehead's—and for no other philosopher has he so much respect. It is this philosophy which today is making a powerful impact on many theologians.

---

[27]See Hartshorne, *Reality as Social Process,* p. 18.

CHAPTER VII

The Divine Dipolarity

We find in the first two lines of a famous hymn a full expression of the union of the two notions [permanence and flux] in one integral experience:

Abide with me;
Fast falls the eventide.

Here the first line expresses the permanences, 'abide,' 'me' and the 'Being' addressed; and the second line sets these permanences amid the inescapable flux. Here at length we find formulated the complete problem of metaphysics.

Alfred North Whitehead[1]

OUR EXCURSION into Hartshorne's thought has revealed the extent of his affinity with Whiteheadian metaphysics. What gives him special importance for our purposes is his concentration on the doctrine of God, to which he has devoted years of painstaking labor. We are now familiar with certain features of his doctrine of God, having examined it as one of the major elements in his philosophy. However, in order to appreciate the relevance of Hartshorne for present-day theological reflection, we require a somewhat fuller treatment of the doctrine. This chapter is intended to fulfill that requirement by taking a fresh tack on his doctrine of God—in particular, by examining his view of what in the theological tradition have been called the divine attributes.

---

[1]From *Process and Reality*, p. 318. Used by permission.

The more full-bodied a doctrine of God, the more it will be relevant to actual religious experience and practice, and hence the more it will be able to illumine actual expressions of religion. Such expressions may very well involve questions of metaphysics. As Whitehead points out in the epigraph above, a famous hymn states in its first two lines the complete problem of metaphysics. In its theological form this problem can be found in many hymns—as well as in prayers, scripture, or creeds.

For example, consider the words of the following hymn, which many of us sing from time to time in services of worship:

"Great is Thy faithfulness," O God my Father,
There is no shadow of turning with Thee;
Thou changest not, Thy compassions, they fail not;
As Thou hast been Thou forever wilt be.

"Great is Thy faithfulness! Great is Thy faithfulness!"
Morning by morning new mercies I see;
All I have needed Thy hand hath provided—
"Great is Thy faithfulness," Lord, unto me![2]

If we examine these words from the point of view of their logic, we become aware that they contain a puzzle. On the one hand, God is regarded as changeless: "There is no shadow of turning with Thee; Thou changest not . . . As Thou hast been Thou forever wilt be." On the other hand, he is regarded as changing: he is fatherly and compassionate, exhibits new mercies morning by morning, and provides for personal need.

How can one who changes not also be compassionate? Can an unmoved being be moved to love and mercy? What father do you know who will forever be as he has been? How can one in whom there is no shadow of turning provide for one's needs, which change throughout his life?

---

[2]Thomas O. Chisholm, author. Copyright by Hope Publishing Co. Used by permission.

Face to face with the problem of God's immutability, it appears that we must make a choice. (1) We may hold—with the mainstream of classical Christian theology—that God is changeless and complete in all respects. If so, he could in no way grow or increase in value, and service to him would be impossible, since he could receive nothing.[3] (2) We may hold—in opposition to the mainstream of classical Christian theology—that God is in no respect changeless and complete. This implies, however, that he changes (or is capable of change) in every way, is therefore unreliable, and might even cease to be recognizable at all. If we must choose between these alternatives, the choice is hardly a pleasant one.

Hartshorne has shown that the problem is not as simple as this,[4] for it may be wrong to assert that God is changeless and complete in all respects, and it may *also* be wrong to assert that he is in no respect changeless and complete. The truth, as Hartshorne says, may lie in a neglected alternative: that God is changeless and complete in *some* respects, but not in all. In short, we may find the truth not by taking one pole to the exclusion of the other but rather by taking both poles in combination. There is no stupefying paradox in this. Indeed, we meet dipolarity on every hand. A boy may spin a top so expertly that for the moment its axis remains steady and fixed. Yet the top rotates about its axis. Hence, it is changeless in one respect, changing in another. To take another example, "ol' man river" as it rolls along is certainly changing. Still, the *fact* that the river flows is itself unchanging (so long as the river continues to flow and is not dammed, frozen, or dried up). Still another example of dipolarity is furnished by our very experience. A man who was sick last week may now be fully recovered. If so, he is not *precisely* the same person he was, for he is no longer ill. None-

---

[3]What is absolutely fixed simply cannot change, whether for better or worse. And what cannot change cannot receive anything, since such reception would constitute a change.

[4]See, for example, Hartshorne, *Reality as Social Process*, pp. 155-162.

theless, in reporting his experience, he suggests that the change has not canceled his identity: "*I* was sick," he tells us. "*I* am now well." Both permanence and change are present—as in all human experience. Man is dipolar.

The principle of dipolarity sheds light on the problem of God's immutability. Let us consider the problem from the point of view of three of his attributes, namely, power, wisdom, and love.

It is perhaps unfortunate that we call God omnipotent. For the term literally means "all-powerful," which suggests that he wields all the power there is or could be. If so, then only God has power and only he could have power. But, as Hartshorne points out,[5] religion has always distinguished between God's power and the power or powers that enact evil. If God possesses all actual and possible power, it follows that he alone is responsible for the evil which has been done and in addition that he alone will be responsible for all future evil. Furthermore, if God has an absolute monopoly on power, over whom can he exercise it? Over you and me? On this theory, you and I are supposed to possess no power whatsoever. Indeed, there is absolutely nothing over which God—as the sole power in the universe—could exercise his power. If, as Hartshorne holds, power is a meaningful concept only if it entails the notion of opposing power—if, that is, power is *in principle* shared—the doctrine that God has limitless power simply does not make sense.[6]

These considerations prompt us to redefine divine omnipotence. We may say that God is omnipotent, not in the sense that he is the cosmic dictator of all things, but in the sense that no other power is or could be as great as his. Reality is a society of greater and lesser powers in interaction with one another, God being the cosmic power to which there could be neither

---

[5]See, for example, Hartshorne, "Omnipotence," *An Encyclopedia of Religion*, ed. Vergilius Ferm (1945), p. 545.

[6]The popular doctrine that God "limits himself," lending some fraction of his power to creatures, involves the supposition that it is theoretically possible for him to possess all power. However, if in the nature of the case power must be shared, this supposition is false and the popular doctrine therefore ill-founded.

an equal nor a superior. He influences the actions of all beings in the universe but does not coerce or fully determine them. This conception of God's omnipotence seems to be what men of religion have ordinarily intended when they spoke of divine power. It allows one to affirm that God's power is unalterable and yet forever at work in the world. It is thus a doctrine of the dipolarity of divine power.

In this new conception, God's power in an important sense is changeless and perfect, but this does not mean that whatever happens is God's doing. Rather, it means that in all circumstances God exercises a cosmic influence which no other could equal or surpass. No being can escape the divine influence, nor could anything destroy it. To speak of the providence of God is to refer to this indestructible greatest possible power among all powers, which sways the others according to its undeviating beneficence. In short, God's power is changeless *in character or quality* though changing in its concrete manifestations.

To the question: "But how can you claim that God is omnipotent when there is so much evil in the world?" the reply is that the questioner has failed to grasp the new definition of God's omnipotence. Though God in principle has supreme power, his is not the only power in the universe. Therefore, things can (and do) occur contrary to his will. In fact, if each of the multiplicity of beings enjoys some power, it is highly unlikely that evil and discord among them can be avoided. As Hartshorne remarks, the fact that God possesses the best possible power does not guarantee the best possible world.[7]

If there is always evil and discord (or at least the likelihood of such) among free creatures, what is the nature of God's providential influence over them? We may suppose that he sets the limits in terms of which freedom operates. Had he placed enough constraint upon freedom to reduce the danger of evil to negligible proportions, opportunities for good would have been re-

---

[7]See Hartshorne, *An Encyclopedia of Religion*, p. 546.

duced in like measure. Parents can protect a child from all risks only at the cost of all opportunities for him. Where there is no risk, there is no opportunity. On the other hand, had God so lessened the constraint upon freedom as to maximize the opportunities for good, risks would likewise have been maximized. Once more, parents can allow a child unrestricted freedom only at great risk to him. Where opportunity is great, so is risk. Presumably, God sets conditions in such a way that the result is neither a tame and harmless order nor a wild and dangerous disorder.[8] Hence, he must provide the right mixture of freedom and constraint, one which affords the maximal surplus of opportunities over risks.

We have discussed God's power mainly in terms of his influence upon the beings in the world. It is natural enough when we think of power to think of the capacity to act. But if God is the supreme power *among others,* what the others do will doubtless have an effect on him. Indeed, the perfection of God's power will involve his capacity to *receive the influences of the world* in the most excellent way. This is certainly no news to men of religious faith. Many philosophers and theologians have insisted that God is impassive, independent of all influences, and therefore really indifferent toward the creatures. Men of religious faith, however, have always believed—in the words of another famous hymn—that God is "only wise" (meaning all wise), that his knowledge is both clear and complete. What, after all, is such knowledge except unqualified *sensitivity* to the influences of the world's beings?

The all-wisdom of God, another of his attributes, is called his omniscience. Divine omniscience implies that for every change in the world there is a corresponding change in God. Accordingly, God's knowledge is relative to (dependent on) the feelings and actions of the beings that compose the world. His knowledge, therefore, cannot be regarded as a changeless, inert

---

[8]See Hartshorne, *The Divine Relativity,* p. 136.

totality. It grows in content, adding new items of knowledge in accordance with every change in the world. But, as stated above, God's reception of influences is an aspect of his omnipotence, not a weakness or defect.

Hartshorne illustrates this point as follows.[9] He asks us to imagine an eloquent poem read in the presence of: (1) a glass of water, (2) an ant, (3) a dog, (4) a person unfamiliar with the language in which the poem is written, (5) a person who knows the language but is insensitive to poetry, and (6) a person who knows the language and is sensitive to poetry as well. The glass of water will scarcely be affected by the reading. The ant may vaguely experience sound waves from the reader. The dog will perhaps sense some of the emotional tones in the reader's voice. The person unfamiliar with the language of the poem will likely be aware of the moods and verbal music of the poem. The one who knows the language but is insensitive to poetry will perhaps grasp ideas and images, but lack aesthetic enjoyment. Finally, he who listens knowingly and appreciatively will experience an adventure in thought and feeling. The series moves from less to more understanding and *at the same time* from less to more dependence on the poem. The power to know is the power to depend on the objects of knowledge.

If in one sense divine knowledge is dependent and changing, in another it is independent and changeless, for our conception of God is dipolar throughout. In the light of what has been said, it is not difficult to see how God's omniscience is independent and changeless, for it always corresponds to its objects. It *always* does so. God's knowledge is constant—unfailing—in its adequacy to its objects. Hence, his knowledge is absolute, complete, changeless in its infallibility.

Thus, we may say that God's knowledge is changeless, not in its content, but in its type or character. If God knows all things with unqualified adequacy, he knows them just as they are—the

---

[9] See *ibid.*, p. 49.

actual as actual, the possible as possible. One reason for making this point is that it bears on the age-old problem of divine foreknowledge. It is sometimes claimed that God, being omniscient, knows all those events which for us are future. Such a theory assumes that the future is composed of events as real, definite, and detailed as those which compose the past. But the future is future precisely because it is *not yet* real, definite, and detailed. If this were not the case, then you and I, and all our descendants would already be dead and buried. The function of time, as Hartshorne remarks, is to settle issues in sequence one by one.[10] If the future is as yet unsettled, that is exactly the way God knows it—as unsettled. If God "knew" it in any other way, he would "know" falsely, for, as we have said, God's knowledge is perfectly adequate to its objects: he knows things as they truly are. The upshot is that God knows the past as finished—settled— in every detail, the present as in process of actualization, and the future as indefinite and yet to be settled.

Since God's knowledge of events is infallible, we may suppose that no event ever slips from the divine memory. Events which we remember vaguely and partially are remembered by God clearly and comprehensively. One way of stating this is to say that each event in the world is destined for immortality in God's memory. Such a doctrine clarifies one of our commonsense notions, namely, that once an event occurs, it will forever after be true that it occurred precisely as it did, for God's memory is the perfectly sensitive receptacle of all occurrences.

God's knowledge of the world is not remote and indirect. He is no spectator of events external to himself; he does not stare at an alien world. Rather, he takes the life of the world into his own life and " 'shares with each creature its actual world.' "[11] Hence, God's knowledge is direct, immediate. If this were not so, it would be subject to such imperfections as inhere in medi-

---

[10]See Hartshorne, *Reality as Social Process*, p. 201.
[11]*Ibid.*, p. 202. See Whitehead, *Process and Reality*, p. 523.

99

ated knowing. Were there objects "outside" God, his knowledge of them would be partly inferential (since indirect) and thus inadequate.[12]

Is there in human experience anything analogous to direct, immediate knowledge? We do share in the experiences of family, friends, and associates, but even so our awareness of their experiences is always pale, fleeting, and incomplete. However, as Hartshorne points out, a man *is* directly related to his own body: there is no instrument or mechanism intervening between his mind and, e.g., the nerves in his arm. He says that however much a man's relation to his body differs from God's relation to the world, there is an obvious similarity between the two relations in respect to directness.[13] Hence, we may say that God is the being whose body is the world. This metaphor not only helps us conceive the intimacy of God's relation to the world, it also illuminates something that Christian faith has seen from the beginning: that God bears in his own life our pain and sorrow. Thus, the conception of God as all wise leads to the conception of God as fellow sufferer (Whitehead), for God knows our pain and sorrow (not just our joy) by *sharing* it. If the omnipotence of God implies his omniscience or sensitive awareness of each of the creatures, his omniscience in turn implies his compassionate suffering.

Those who insist on the absolute changelessness of God will have particular difficulty with our third topic, the doctrine of divine love, for how can we conceive a being in all respects complete and immutable, a being without need, desire, or feeling, who at the same time loves the creatures? Such a conception involves poor logic and is bound to lead to distortions in religion. Love is nothing less than desire for the good of others, as Hartshorne says.[14] It is a matter of willing their well-being and happi-

---

[12]"The external, it appears, is known by signs which are internal [to the knower], that is, it is known imperfectly, abstractly, partially." Charles Hartshorne, *Man's Vision of God* (Chicago: Willett, Clark & Company, 1941), p. 289.

[13]See *ibid.*, p. 179.

[14]See *ibid.*, p. 14.

ness. But, as before, our conception is dipolar. There is a change-less aspect to the divine love, for its *character* is constant. Charles Wesley wrote:

> Jesus, Thou art all compassion,
> Pure, unbounded love Thou art.

The love of God is like that—all compassion, pure and un-bounded. His love is pure: it is not mixed with indifference or hardness of heart. His love is unbounded: none can "drift be-yond His love and care." The outstretched arms of the crucified Man of Nazareth are an apt symbol for the all-inclusiveness of the divine love. It is the character of God's love, so conceived, that is immutable.

Our love for one another is neither pure nor unbounded. Self-interest always inhibits our wishes for others, and ignorance radi-cally limits our awareness of them. God, being omniscient, knows all actual beings as parts of his own life. It follows that God, in willing your good or mine or any creature's, *also wills his own*. Thus, in God, there is an absolute coincidence of self-interest and other-interest.

When we do good for others, we are always partly ignorant of the good we accomplish. Indeed, a man may be long dead before good he was instrumental in bringing about is realized. But God is deathless, and every beauty and joy he enables us to have becomes an element in his own experience. Hence, there is for God no question of seeking the good of the creatures to the exclusion of his own good. Nor, on the other hand, is there for God any question of seeking his own good in disregard of the creatures' good.[15] Both statements are true for the same reason: the good God intends for the creature is at the same time his very own good.

---

[15]Of course, the good that God seeks and realizes may fail to include the good (the genuine good) a creature wishes for itself, not because God is indifferent to its good—indeed, he suffers the sorrow and loss involved—but because he cannot avoid selection among conflicting and incompatible forms of good.

Recall that in a metaphorical sense the world is God's body. A person's well-being is the well-being of his bodily members, and conversely their well-being is his. If my wife gives me a pair of slippers on my birthday and someone contends that she did not give *me* the slippers but rather gave them to my feet, the reply is obvious: she benefited me precisely by benefiting my feet.

It is *because* God's love is forever changeless in character that its concrete content and expression differ from person to person, and from situation to situation. We find illustration of this point in human love. A parent's love for his children is constant only if his thoughts, feelings, and actions are tailored to each child at each stage of that child's life. We may assume that the father in Jesus' parable of the prodigal did not love the one son more than the other. Yet in order for his love to remain true and constant, it had to correspond in its concrete content and expression to the differences between the two sons.

God loves the neighbor (that is, the creature) with the same intimacy with which he (God) loves himself, for in God self-interest and other-interest are absolutely coincident. Since God loves us and desires our good, he experiences sorrow when conflict and suffering befall us. Hence, God's love by no means guarantees his unqualified happiness. The good man, as Hartshorne reminds us, suffers more intensely than the bad at the spectacle of suffering and evil in others.[16] The defeat of our interests is the defeat of God's *own* interests[17] and constitutes an element of tragedy within the divine life.

The doctrine that God joys in our joys and sorrows in our sorrows has important ethical implications. For example, there are in our day thousands of people who desperately need education, housing, job opportunities, etc. If our doctrine of God's love tells us anything at all, it tells us that when we deny these

---

[16]See Hartshorne, *Man's Vision of God*, p. 14.

[17]This does not mean that God shares the morally evil "interests" of creatures and is therefore himself wicked. Hartshorne regards moral evil as privative: it is not interest; it is *lack* of interest.

people, we deny God; that when we treat them with fairness and concern, we serve God, for what we do "to one of the least of these"[18] we do to God himself. We have all been reared on the idea that God is father and all men brothers. This concept is pale and abstract beside the truth that my fellow man is "a very fragment of the life of God."[19] We are members one of another because we are members of the living whole, which is unified by divine love.

God, on this interpretation, does not stand off and merely wish us well, nor is his love merely eagerness to do things for us. Divine love is instead sympathetic identification with us in our sufferings as well as in our joys. It is important to note that sympathetic identification does not mean endorsement of all our purposes and desires. In the nature of the case, God could not endorse those which are evil. But even among those purposes and desires that are not evil, he must choose some and reject others, for his sway upon the world must take some direction or other—not all directions at once. Doubtless he chooses in such a way that the greatest possible good is realized. In any event, our interests are never discarded as irrelevant or impertinent. Indeed, God passively wishes, that is, he feels with and for all creatures, what they wish for themselves,[20] but he must resolve the conflict of interests which he thus takes upon himself. He will not resolve it in such a way as to rob us of all freedom. Consequently, he suffers a double tragedy: he is unable to realize the multifarious interests which he endorses, and he must endure cruel and insensitive feelings, thoughts, and acts, which he does not endorse.

Hartshorne's doctrine of God represents a clear and cogent statement of the religious man's understanding of God. Christian theology, where it has been under the influence of Greek metaphysics, has always leaned toward a conception of God which

---

[18]Matt. 25:40b.
[19]Hartshorne, *Reality as Social Process*, pp. 151-152.
[20]See Hartshorne, *Man's Vision of God*, p. 293.

subordinates and even disregards certain fundamental religious insights, a conception in which God is viewed as utterly changeless and complete in all respects. What Hartshorne shows (indirectly) is that the biblical picture of God is far more respectable philosophically than theologies which, though wrought by the wisest of men, are in the grip of the conception of God as static completion. Conceiving God as a dipolarity of permanence and flux, he provides a rational interpretation of the God of Abraham, Isaac, and Jacob—and of Jesus—a rational interpretation of the God whose power, while unsurpassable, is social; whose wisdom, while perfect, is ever changing; and whose love, while constant, is pure sensitivity to creaturely joy and sorrow.

CHAPTER VIII

A Framework for Christian Thought

> *Now a philosophical theology which takes process as its basic category has one supreme advantage over the metaphysical systems in which Christian thought has traditionally been expressed. This philosophy makes it possible for the Living God, the God who acts, the caring, saving God of the Bible to be made intelligible. . . . To think of God as acting in dynamic relation to His creatures not merely as one actor among many, but as the universal creative power which sustains all things, and without which they could neither be nor act, is true to what our best knowledge of the world tells us. It is true to the insight of the Bible, which the philosophical tradition has tended to obscure behind the impassive mask of absolute, static being.*
>
> Daniel Day Williams[1]

UP TO THIS POINT, our aim has been to achieve an understanding of metaphysics, particularly of the process metaphysics represented by Whitehead and Hartshorne. Process metaphysics may very well prove to be one of the most powerful resources available to Christian theologians of the twentieth century, and in this chapter we wish to turn directly to the question of the relevance of process metaphysics for Christian thought. It is important to be realistic in our expectations of a metaphysical system. There is no reason to expect, for example, that process metaphysics will provide a systematic theology and thus do the theologian's work for him. Indeed, it *cannot* do so—any more than it can do the work of the biologist, the poet, or the statesman. The metaphysician, as you will recall, depends for basic data on the experience, insights, and theories of specialists

---

[1]From *God's Grace and Man's Hope* (New York: Harper & Row, Publishers, 1949), p. 42. Used by permission.

in the sciences and humanities. He himself as metaphysician could not produce such experience, insights, and theories simply because he is working with (or toward) concepts which apply to any existing thing whatsoever, and there is no possibility of leaping from such general concepts to special kinds of things or to particular facts.

The metaphysician does not operate in a vacuum, isolated from every context, but draws upon particular areas of thought or experience to provide him clues to the whole of reality. Convinced that such and such facts are basic, he undertakes to generalize these facts, to give them—perhaps in a revised form—an applicability far beyond their ordinary boundaries. There can be little doubt that the Judeo-Christian heritage has been a resource for process philosophy, a resource of concept, imagery, and insight that, as surely as science, art, history, or philosophy has informed and guided process thinkers.

If the process thinker, like any metaphysician, proceeds by descriptive generalization, if he cannot possibly reverse the methodology and descend by some logical trick from the general to the special or to the particular, it is nonetheless true that all experience is received and interpreted in terms of some theoretical framework. Intelligence functions to uncover the structure or organization of experience, and it is a fair question whether experience is even possible where no structure or organization is discerned or whether, if such experience is possible, it could have the slightest meaning. In any event, a metaphysical system can be regarded as the widest framework of interpretation one can bring to his world.

A Christian theologian operating within the framework of process philosophy will view the world, despite all its variety and diversity, as a single, structured whole, each of its fundamental entities being occasions of experience. This means among other things that the process theologian will reject supernaturalism; he will deny that there is another—perhaps a wholly different—order or realm outside the world in which he exists.

All realities, he holds, share with one another a kinship so that no absolute barrier divides any of them from all the rest.

Process metaphysics is not the doctrine that the world is nothing but a rational system, but it is the doctrine that the world is at least a rational system. There is no escaping the world order, even for God. Indeed, Whitehead declares that God is no exception to the metaphysical principles but is rather "their chief exemplification."[2] Thus, the process theologian will not speak of miraculous, divine intervention in the world. He will try to conceive creation, incarnation, resurrection, and so forth, not as bewildering acts of God, which have no affinity with the structures and processes of the experienced world; rather, he will conceive these as expressions in mythical or symbolic form of facts which, however religiously profound, are yet within the warp and woof of the world's single order. He will not use the Bible as a text in science and cosmology—for as such it is incompatible with his process world view (and besides the Bible is not that kind of book)—but he will accept it as the basic source of religious illumination and inspiration, and avail himself of every resource of biblical scholarship in order to discover its religious intent and significance. The process theologian stands within the liberal tradition of Christian thought, for while he is a man of faith, he holds that faith does not call for sacrifice of the intellect but rather demands to be made intelligible to the modern mind, a demand he seeks to fulfill within the framework of process metaphysics.

Much of the strength of process theology lies precisely in its rejection of otherworldliness. Insistence that God is "wholly other" tends to paralyze theological curiosity and inquiry. No one should be expected to suppress questions as to the meaning of religious doctrine and simply "take things on faith." A man needs to understand as clearly as possible what is meant by God's action in history, by his providential guidance, his self-revealing, his suffering and redeeming. To reply simply that

---

[2]Whitehead, *Process and Reality*, p. 521.

God's ways are past finding out is to give a stone where bread is needed. Indeed, the required nourishment can be given only when theology appeals by analogy to structures, processes, or relations discoverable within human experience.

For example, theologians for centuries have spoken of the grace of God active in the hearts of men. They have spoken of the Holy Spirit moving in the world, particularly among the people of God. How is one to construe the divine influence so that it makes sense in terms of what one knows about the causal network of the world or, to be more specific, so that it makes sense in terms of what one knows about physio-chemical, biological, psychological, sociological, political, and economic processes? Process theology, with is panpsychism and its doctrine of universal relatedness, can answer such questions by reference to factors in the relation between God and the world which bear analogy to factors in the relation between a man and his body, in short, by reference to factors which by analogy have counterparts in concrete human experience. Of course, theologians have always used personal imagery in describing God, have spoken of God as a loving father, have viewed the relation between God and man as a covenant, and so forth. Although such analogies between God and man have been helpful, they have not proved sufficient. Furthermore, there has been in theology a countertendency to the conception of God as personal, a tendency to regard God as radically unlike his creatures and (at least in some theologies) beyond any ascription whatsoever. This countertendency characterizes the mainstream of classical Christian theology.

Whitehead says that the ancient Christian theologians exhibited metaphysical imagination when they decided for the immanence of God in Christ and also when they decided for the immanence of God as Holy Spirit in the world generally.[3] However, "the nature of God was exempted from all the metaphysical categories which applied to the individual things in this

---

[3]See Whitehead, *Adventures of Ideas*, pp. 216-217.

temporal world."[4] This exemption resulted in a gulf between God and world, and "the worst of a gulf is, that it is very difficult to know what is happening on the further side of it."[5] Unfortunately, theological symbols can never convey us across a gulf separating us from utter mystery; therefore, one such symbol is no more appropriate to that mystery than another— or than none at all. Theologians have at times asserted that *no* term can be truly predicated of the Deity, but if that be so, he cannot be distinguished from nothing at all.

The problem of a divine being who transcends the metaphysical structure is a serious one. With respect to theological language, the problem is that no matter which words we choose, their meanings are grounded in the context of human thought and experience, and therefore they are inappropriate—indeed, they are meaningless—when applied to a being discontinuous with that context. With respect to theological knowledge, the problem is that God, if he transcends the metaphysical structure, is inaccessibly beyond our knowing or finding out, in which case we must resign ourselves to unrelieved agnosticism.

The process theologian, in taking the tack that there is a single world order, for God as well as creatures, escapes the problems inherent in otherworldliness and enjoys the advantage of being able to anchor his theological reflection in human thought and experience. But the procedure of the process theologian involves its own set of problems, not the least of which is the problem of anthropomorphism, for if God is part of the scheme of things, further, if he is literally a being of power, wisdom, and love, is he not an exalted man rather than the Deity? This problem always dogs a theologian who finds analogy between the divine and the human. As Hartshorne conceives it, the divine-human analogy is between whole and part, not between two parts. For God is the all-inclusive being—and in this sense is being-itself rather than one being among others. Although

[4]*Ibid.*, p. 216.
[5]*Ibid.*, p. 217.

there is analogy between God and man, there is also difference, in principle. For Hartshorne, God differs from man precisely in respect to those characteristics wherein he is also somehow like man.

Some philosophers have argued against theism on the grounds that the theist claims an analogy between God and the human mind but destroys the alleged analogy by denying that God has a body.[6] Hartshorne does nothing of the sort; he affirms that the world is to God as a man's body is to himself. God is distinctive not only in that there is nothing outside his "body"— nothing of which he is only indirectly aware—but also in that he is perfect in his awareness of and influence over that body. It follows "that theology (so far as it is the theory of the essence of deity) is *the most literal* of all sciences of existence."[7] Indeed, it is when we deal with man and the other creatures that literalness is inappropriate, for man and the other creatures always embody characteristics ambiguously, approximately.

Consider human knowledge. We say we know various things, but in each case our "knowledge" turns out to be something less than certain and conclusive; it is always a matter of more or less. But how far short of certainty and conclusiveness can one fall and still possess knowledge? Evidently, human "knowledge" has no exact or definite meaning. The case is different with divine knowledge, for God simply *knows*. His knowledge is utterly infallible, so that when we say God knows X, we mean this without qualification, that is, literally.

The same is true of the other psychical conceptions. While in some vague sense they apply to man, they apply to God simply and literally. A man may be said to love his neighbor, but not quite, or at least with this or that qualification. God loves— period. A man remembers some fragments of the past. God remembers—period. A man may be said to endure, but only for a

---

[6] See Hartshorne, *Beyond Humanism*, p. 255.

[7] Hartshorne, *The Divine Relativity*, p. 36. Italics added. This does not deny the need for symbolic speech about God. God is not literally a shepherd, a lord, or a father. But such usage does not belong to the pure theory of the divine essence.

time. God endures—period. "In this sense, it is the theistic use only of psychical conceptions which has literal meaning, a meaning from which all other meanings are derived by qualification, diminution, or negation."[8] Thus, in regard to qualities wherein man is like God, divine eminence is preserved in principle, God being the standard by which all human embodiments of those qualities must be measured. This implies that we can arrive at knowledge of ourselves (and hence at a knowledge of our own defects) only to the extent that we attain a knowledge of God. Hartshorne observes: "Our own natures it is which (partially) negate the categories, not God's [nature]."[9] He, in his essence, is their literal embodiment or, in Whitehead's words, "their chief exemplification." The affirmation of analogy between God and man need not make God in the image of man. Hartshorne has shown that though we find in man—and the other creatures—an analogue to the divine attributes, we are not obliged to identify divine with human nature but may conceive each as distinct (in principle) from the other.

Since the categories apply unambiguously to God and to him alone, they constitute his individuality, that is, they define his identity as God. The implication is not only that God has a metaphysically unique status and character (as we have said) but that he can in his individuality or Godhood be conceived a priori.[10] Your individuality or mine is not definable a priori, that is, solely by reference to universal categories. Your individuality or mine, being a particular instance of characteristics shared by multitudes, cannot be known simply by reason but must be experienced or felt as an empirical fact. But God, because the categories *are* his individuality, is known, however indistinctly, to the extent that anyone is aware of those all-pervasive structures (categories) sought by the metaphysician.

It is evident that the process theologian must reject exclusive

---

[8]Hartshorne, *The Logic of Perfection,* p. 141.
[9]Hartshorne, *The Divine Relativity,* p. 36.
[10]See *Ibid.,* p. 31.

Christocentrism, which involves the doctrine that man can know God only through Christ. Respecting this point, two observations are especially relevant. First, one would be hard pressed to make a case for this doctrine on scriptural grounds. Indeed, as Schubert Ogden, an American process theologian and Bultmann scholar, asserts,

Paul's conviction, like that of Scripture as a whole, is that men are utterly and radically responsible because God has always made himself known to them as gracious Father and has thereby deprived them of all excuse for their self-willed estrangement from his holy presence.[11]

In referring to "Paul's conviction," Ogden has in mind particularly Romans 1:18-21, where Paul insists that men who have failed to honor God or give him thanks cannot claim ignorance of him and thus be excused, for "they knew God." Ogden points out that when Paul speaks of the revelation of God "in the things that have been made" (Romans 1:20), he is referring not merely to the "concept of God" or to the "question concerning God" or to a purely "negative knowledge" or, in general, to something less than full knowledge of God. "On the contrary," says Ogden, "he affirms simply that 'what can be known about God is plain to them, because God has shown it to them' [Romans 1:19] and so leaves no doubt that the content of this primordial revelation is precisely identical with the 'new' knowledge now to be laid hold of in the 'obedience of faith.' "[12]

Second, a doctrine of God, so far as it is Christian (that is, so far as it is based on Jesus Christ), will necessarily be in accord with the understanding of God in process thought. God cannot be disclosed in or through a person if he (God) utterly transcends the categories. Indeed, a Christian doctrine of God, far from representing the Deity as "wholly other," will scarcely avoid anthropomorphism. Of course, classical theologians avoided

---

[11]Schubert M. Ogden, *Christ Without Myth* (New York: Harper & Row, Publishers, 1961), p. 142. Used by permission.

[12]*Ibid.* Used by permission.

112

anthropomorphism by affirming that Christ, though one in person, possessed two natures, the one divine and the other human. They were correct in denying a simple unity (or identity) between God and the human Jesus, for although there is unity between God and man, there is also difference. However, the classical Christological formulations were inadequate. No person can have two natures and still be one person.[13] In any event, a Christian doctrine of God must rest somehow on the history of Jesus—on his preaching and acts of healing; on his associations with fishermen, Pharisees, harlots, tax collectors, and all the rest; and on his eventual death on a cross. It is a history which conveys unmistakably the impression of steadfastness and courage, but above all of suffering love. It is therefore a history which for the Christian symbolizes nothing less than the love of God himself, for " 'greater love has no man than this, that a man lay down his life for his friends.' " For the process theologian, the doctrine of divine love, sublimely symbolized in the life of Jesus, is the center about which all other considerations revolve. Insofar, process theism stands squarely within Christian faith.

Still, if the divine essence is known to the extent that the categories are known, and further, if no human being can exemplify the categories eminently, can Jesus be regarded as the once-and-for-all, decisive, and normative disclosure of God? Ogden has sought to work out a Christology by employing the analogy that the world is to God as a man's body is to himself. His thesis is that while all of one's bodily actions are his own, since to some extent they result from the inner decisions by which he constitutes himself a person or a self, some of his bodily actions, especially in interpersonal relations, are *peculiarly his own*. "Such actions are, as we say, our 'characteristic' actions, for in them or through them the persons we are, are uniquely

---

[13]As we have seen, it *is* possible for two persons (personally ordered societies) to possess the same categorial nature, though one possess it eminently and the other noneminently or deficiently. The unity and difference between God and man is to be understood in this way.

re-presented or revealed to others."[14] In an analogous fashion, while all creatures are in one sense God's own acts, certain creaturely happenings may be said to be his acts in a special sense— a possibility "peculiarly open to those uniquely human events in which man expresses his understanding of the ultimate meaning of his existence through symbolic speech and action."[15] Since Jesus, in both word and act, expresses the ultimate truth about human existence, namely, the truth that we are created and redeemed by God's sovereign love, Jesus himself is God's decisive act. "For in him, in the word that he speaks and is, God's action as Creator and Redeemer is expressed with utter decisiveness."[16]

Provocative as all this is, I am not persuaded that it is a satisfactory account of the decisiveness of Jesus Christ, nor do I suppose that Ogden is entirely content with it. (1) One act of God is neither more nor less characteristic of him than any other such act; his acts are never "out of character." It is we men who reveal ourselves in a special, definitive way only in certain acts. God acts "as Creator and Redeemer" in every case, not just on occasion. Indeed, if—as Ogden holds—Jesus' history reveals "that all things have their beginning and end in God's pure unbounded love,"[17] then Jesus' history is an affirmation that God acts *at all times and places* in his characteristic, divine way. (2) While no creature escapes the persuasive influence of God, every creature enjoys a measure of autonomy, and in man autonomy is in principle at a maximum. It follows that a man's feelings, decisions, thoughts, interpretations, words, and deeds are in part his own and cannot in a strict sense be identified as *God's* acts. Moreover, it may be argued that man, because of his situation as a creature, acts in ways that are simply not open to God. For example, Jesus may resist temptation, but God, who is free of

---

[14]Ogden, "What Sense Does it Make to Say, 'God Acts in History'?" *The Journal of Religion*, XLIII (January, 1963), p. 14.

[15]*Ibid.*, p. 15.

[16]*Ibid.*, p. 17.

[17]*Ibid.*

temptation, cannot. Resistance to temptation, then, is Jesus' act—but not God's. (3) If, as Ogden has it, God can act in history to reveal himself in a special sense, he can do so in various times and places. Hence, there is no reason to suppose that in Jesus we have the criterion "by which all putative revelations are at once judged and fulfilled."[18] Indeed, Ogden himself lays the ax to this alleged criterion when he accepts the Pauline doctrine that the content of God's self-disclosure "in the things that have been made" is precisely identical with his self-disclosure in Jesus.

Ogden must be pressed to explain why, if Jesus expresses in word and deed a particular understanding of our life before God, it follows that he is the decisive act of God. One could not draw this conclusion unless on other grounds he already knew the character of God and his relation to man. On the other hand, if on other grounds one knew the character of God and his relation to man, this knowledge, not Jesus, would be decisive—and the only conclusion to be drawn would be that by this criterion the particular understanding of our life before God expressed by Jesus in word and deed is valid.[19]

This problem demands further consideration. A man must already know God in order to know that Jesus truly reveals him and is therefore decisive. But if one already knows God, it is this knowledge that is decisive, not the revelation in Jesus' history. Perhaps it will be said that one does not *know* that Jesus truly reveals God but only *believes* that he does; that consequently there is no reason to suppose a prior knowledge of God. It follows, of course, that then one does not *know* that Jesus is decisive but only *believes* that he is. But the belief that Jesus is the decisive disclosure of God rests on prior belief about God.

---

[18]*Ibid.*, p. 16.

[19]The German theologian Rudolf Bultmann holds that though knowledge of authentic existence (that is, existence in faith) is available outside Christianity, Jesus is nonetheless decisive, since he bestows the factual possibility of living authentically. Ogden denies this latter contention, charging that Bultmann is here offering a mythological interpretation of Jesus. While this is true, it may be doubted whether Ogden succeeds in his attempt to account for the decisiveness of Jesus.

(Otherwise, why should a person not believe a quite different sort of man to be the decisive disclosure of God? Or, why should he not believe that Jesus is the decisive disclosure of a nondivine being—or, possibly, no disclosure at all?) Such a prior belief about God, however, would itself be decisive, since it would constitute the criterion by which to judge the disclosure of God in Jesus.

In general, it seems that one must possess some notion of God—some knowledge or belief about God—before Jesus can become known to him as the revelation of God. In Jesus a man becomes acquainted with something he already knows, at least to some extent, or with something he already believes.

For the process theologian, God is known insofar as the categories or metaphysical principles are known, for they define God's essence. Since (as we have said) no man can exemplify the categories eminently, Jesus, like any creature, can manifest God's nature only in an approximate way. In short, he is not decisive in the sense that he embodies the divine essence. Perhaps, however, he is decisive in some other sense, for the essence or nature of God is not God in his fullness—in his concreteness, in his actual states of experience. Although we may know God (in his essence or nature) with our minds, our words and concepts forever fail to express the divine fullness, which we but dimly feel. Reversing a traditional theological affirmation, we may say that understanding seeks faith. That is, understanding, in order to compensate for its own abstractness and thereby do some justice to the concreteness of its object, seeks an incarnate expression of its insights into the divine. The fullness of God, vaguely sensed, can be appropriately represented only by the concrete itself—ideally by a human being (for God is a personally ordered society of occasions, that is, a person, in Whitehead's technical sense). Christians have discerned in Jesus the most adequate means of symbolizing the divine concreteness. He is a symbol not in speech, thought, or art but in historical fact: a living symbol of the living God. To say then that Jesus is decisive is to say something like this: "The living God—though

116

possessed of a character no man can possess—is imaged in the Man of Nazareth with a fullness and power that I find incomparable." Jesus is a language about God which for Christians speaks most faithfully and truthfully of its object. He is not the word (at least, not *the* word) of God to man but the word, in and through a man, about God.

If the process theologian has not yet struggled through to an adequate Christology, he is doubtless in company with most theologians who take seriously modern advances in man's knowledge and understanding of the world, and who can therefore no longer employ the traditional, orthodox formulations. Obviously, an exclusive Christocentrism, which proclaims that God is known only through Jesus Christ, is not an option for the process theologian, for whom even the humblest creature is related, however vaguely, to God. The process doctrine of God's immanence in all creatures, although it may pose problems for some forms of Christology, represents an insight of the highest importance for Christian theology. Process thought construes divine immanence in analogy with concrete human experience (in particular, in analogy with the body's relation to the mind) and is thereby able to clarify not only the meaning of God's omnipresence but also the sense in which God creatively rules the world. Never before has divine providence been explained so plainly and persuasively. Once a man sees that the world is composed of occasions of experience, he can understand that God—the universal datum—communicates his desires to the creatures by virtue of their own psychic participation in him, just as a human being in an analogous way communicates his desires to the cells in his body. We may say, therefore, that each creature knows God with an immediate love and through this relation to God is guided by the inspiration of his aims and intentions for it. In this sense, God is creator. This does not imply that creatures are without freedom, for within the context of God's directives for it, each creature is self-determining.

A second theme of process thought which has special relevance for Christian theology is that, while God is immanent in the creatures, they are at the same time immanent in him. If the first theme illumines the meaning of God's providential guidance of the world, the second illumines the meaning of his knowledge, love, and suffering, in a word, his sensitivity to the world. "There are," says Hartshorne, "no gradations in the intimacy of things to God."[20] Or more vividly: "God has nowhere to hide himself from any sorrow or joy whatever, but must share in all the wealth and all the burden of the world."[21] Though this doctrine is deeply rooted in scripture, it has at times been resisted by theologians, since it implies that God is relative to or dependent on the creatures. The process theologian frankly and gladly accepts this implication. After all, inability to be influenced (impassivity, as it has been called) is nothing but inability to take account of others, which in one context means ignorance and in another, indifference. Far from exhibiting impassivity, God, since he is omniscient and omnibenevolent, is eminently passive or sensitive. A man's awareness of his own body furnishes the best analogue to the divine passivity. While such awareness is direct, and in this respect Godlike, it is indistinct and of course limited to one tiny fragment of the total universe, and in these respects is un-Godlike. By virtue of his unqualified passivity, God includes in himself all things precisely as they are. This means that no man sorrows alone and that none rejoices alone. It means, as Hartshorne observes, that "to wish something is to wish that God might be or have something; to regret something is to regret that God is or has it. All functions are God-functions."[22] It means that in God there is tragedy and suffering—an insight to be found in both the Old and the New Testaments.

A third theme of importance to Christian theology follows directly from the second. All events, since they are known in-

[20]Hartshorne, *Man's Vision of God*, p. 199.

[21]*Ibid.*, p. 198.

[22]Hartshorne, "The Idea of God—Literal or Analogical?" *The Christian Scholar*, XXXIX (June, 1956), 135.

fallibly by God, are preserved or retained in his life everlast-
ingly. They are immortalized in the divine memory. This doctrine, according to Ogden, provides "a way to demythologize
[that is, give the inner religious intent rather than the outward,
mythological meaning of] such important theological notions
as 'resurrection' and 'everlasting life.' "[23] In addition, the doctrine suggests what is meant by the concept of God as redeemer.
As Ogden puts it, to say that God acts as redeemer is to say

that the final destiny both of myself and of all my fellow creatures
is to contribute ourselves not only to the self-creation of the subsequent
worlds of creatures but also to the self-creation of God, who accepts
us without condition into his own everlasting life, where we have a
final standing or security that can nevermore be lost.[24]

Thus, in receiving and conserving all things, God is the redeemer of all, just as in communicating his desires to all things,
he is the creator of all. Here again we appeal to concrete human
experience to provide an analogue by which to conceive God;
indeed, the only process we know by which the past is preserved
is memory—though in God memory has an eminent form (is
complete and accurate), while in man (and other creatures)
it is always deficient.

A fourth theme comes to mind: that of creaturely freedom
and responsibility, for if God is the perfectly sensitive recipient
of every event, he does not fully determine them and therefore
some power of decision or enactment resides in each event.
Process thought not only takes seriously the concept that "creation continues"; it sees creativity as the most fundamental of
metaphysical principles and hence characteristic of every individual reality. It follows that the creatures are also creators.
Of course, God has created us. But, as Hartshorne says, if he
"has created even our decisions, then in what sense are they

---

[23]Ogden, "Theology and Philosophy: A New Phase of the Discussion," *The Journal
of Religion*, XLIV (January, 1964), 5.
[24]Ogden. *The Journal of Religion*, XLIII, 12. Used by permission of The University of Chicago Press, publisher.

our decisions?"[25] God determines the creature only in part, leaving at least some alternatives for its own determination. Man enjoys far greater freedom than does any other creature. He "is capable of departing widely from his proper place in the scheme of things, making himself, as it were, less than a man."[26] At worst, man arrogates to himself functions and privileges that belong only to God. "We should like to seem infallible, omnipotent, absolutely righteous, at least in some sphere."[27]

Of course, process theologians are aware of an ancient theological truth, "that somehow it is deeply natural to man to prefer the lesser or narrower to the greater or more generous objective."[28] To some extent, this tendency qualifies human freedom and thus human responsibility. Hence, the old question is raised: Is man really capable of the good, or is he morally weak-kneed and therefore dependent on God's grace? The process theologian, though he does not gloss over man's natural tendency to sin, insists in his answer to this question (1) that human freedom is never inoperative or inconsequential—so long as one is in command of his faculties—and (2) that, however extensive his freedom may be, man can never act apart from the sustaining power of God. Although we cannot of our own strength rise to full human stature, we can of our own strength—that is, consciously and willingly—accept "the operation in us of the love which infinitely transcends but inspires our own."[29] It is important to recognize that full human stature is never divine stature, that our love is forever less than perfect.

But the sense that we cannot love as God loves, while it humiliates us, may also "save" us from failure to love as we can. To fill one's mind with the thought of the divine, not as coldly perfect or blandly benevolent, but as tragically sympathetic, more at one with us in our

[25]Hartshorne, "A Philosopher's Assessment of Christianity," *Religion and Culture: Essays in Honor of Paul Tillich,* ed. Walter Leibrecht (New York: Harper & Row, Publishers, 1959), p. 168.

[26]*Ibid.,* p. 179.

[27]Hartshorne, *Reality as Social Process,* p. 149.

[28]*Ibid.*

[29]*Ibid.,* pp. 149-150.

grief than we can be with each other, or even with our own past experiences (which we, but not God, have largely forgotten) is to find selfish desires and pride losing some of their charm.[30]

The discussion of creaturely freedom and responsibility presupposes the relatedness of creatures and thus suggests a fifth theme with theological relevance, namely, that each individual is a dipolar, mental-physical unity. The relation among creatures is never a purely spiritual affair—as though creatures (at least the most exalted) were pure, nonbodily spirits in communion with one another. Williams has this point in mind when he remarks that much of the talk about the "I-Thou" relationship dodges the really hard problems. "We are not disincarnate spirits in 'I-Thou' relations," he says. "We are human beings embedded in organic and physical processes, and the mystery of man is how the 'I-Thou' relationship appears *in this setting*."[31]

Of course, one's relation to another creature is not merely a relation to another particular, localized mental-physical unity; it is at the same time a relation to God himself—in accordance with the second theme. This solves the ostensible puzzle as to how one could love the neighbor *in addition* to God if he were to love God (as the Christian is commanded) with *all* his heart, mind, soul, and strength, for the neighbor is not "in addition to God," but literally included within his very life. "That other fellow (of whatever social class) whose sonship to God we may abstractly admit, is not just a product of divine power, or just an object of divine well-wishing, but a very fragment of the life of God which is made all-inclusive through sympathy."[32] At last it is clear why, if we do or fail to do to "the least of these," we also do or fail to do to God.

The process view that man (like other creatures) is a mental-physical unity represents a restatement of the Hebraic under-

---

[30]*Ibid.*, p. 150. Used by permission.

[31]Daniel D. Williams, "Christianity and Naturalism: An Informal Statement," *Union Seminary Quarterly Review*, XII (May, 1957), p. 52. Italics added.

[32]Hartshorne, *Reality as Social Process*, pp. 151-152. Used by permission.

standing of man, which is best expressed in the Old Testament. The view is at odds with the Greek conception of man as a soul, temporarily and accidentally associated with a body. On the Greek interpretation of human nature, the doctrine that man is made in the image of God really makes sense only if God is conceived as a soul; on the Hebraic interpretation of human nature, that doctrine really makes sense only if God is conceived as a psychic-somatic unity—as, of course, he is in process theology.

This account of process themes having special relevance for Christian theology is by no means exhaustive. Perhaps it suggests the richness of process philosophy as a context or framework for theological thought. In any event, process philosophy represents a new alternative for the theological world, one which renders obsolete many an old discussion of theology's relation to philosophy, for certain stereotypes regarding the structure and limits of philosophy are now seen to be premature and arbitrary in light of the achievements of the process philosophers. Because of the new situation afforded by process philosophy, theology has the opportunity to enter a new phase in its relation with philosophy; indeed, it has a golden opportunity.

CHAPTER IX

Retrospect and Prospect

> *The notion of a sphere of human knowledge characterized*
> *by unalloyed truth is the pet delusion of dogmatists, whether*
> *they be theologians, scientists, or humanistic scholars.*
>
> Alfred North Whitehead[1]

A NUMBER of American theologians are laboring to forge an alliance between process philosophy and Christian theology. We may with good reason be enthusiastic about the prospect of such an alliance, but at the same time we must take account of certain difficulties and problems relating to process thought.

To many a layman, philosophy is something carried on in an ivory tower far from the traffic of everyday existence, a kind of intellectual chess game about which sensible heads could not care less. We need not take such a caricature seriously except insofar as it suggests one fact worthy of attention: that by nature philosophy is abstract, for the philosopher (that is, the metaphysician) is seeking to devise a scheme of ideas having universal applicability. The charge that philosophers reduce reality to idea or system or reason and thereby crowd out the unpredictable and mysterious is simply unfounded. But how

---

[1]From *Modes of Thought*, p. 94. Used by permission.

is philosophy, which is by nature abstract, capable of presenting things in their concreteness? A concrete reality is always unique, irreplaceable, something more than we can ever capture in any system of classification. Let us consider, for example, my car. It is a blue Ford sedan with eight cylinders, stick shift, and white sidewalls; it is five years old, has 65,000 miles to its credit, and at present needs a wash job. Does any such description (which could of course be extended to some length) really succeed in identifying the car in its concreteness? And if not, could a highly abstract philosophical system possibly be expected to do so? The problem would not be vexing if we could say simply that philosophical categories define the general meaning of concreteness—though they fail to present anything concrete. Whitehead seems to have a slightly different view of the matter. He tells us that philosophy, in one of its functions, is the critic of abstractions, that it not only harmonizes abstractions but *completes them by appealing to concrete fact.*[2] One wonders if Whitehead can really mean this, for it would appear that philosophy, precisely because concrete fact escapes it, is itself incomplete.

The matter is partially cleared up if we take account of what Whitehead means by "concrete." Let us return for a moment to the illustration about the car. From Whitehead's point of view, the trouble with the illustration is that a car is not an example of a concrete fact. What is really illustrated (though unwittingly) in the very supposition that a car is a concrete fact is the Fallacy of Misplaced Concreteness: mistaking the abstract for the concrete. The car is a (nonpersonal) society of occasions of experience, and *these* are the concrete facts. In advancing from the car as a gross, macroscopic object in the garage to the car as a society of occasions, we have (for Whitehead) advanced from abstract conceptualization to concrete conceptualization. Evidently, concrete conceptualization is to be viewed as that level of analysis where not only the elemental

---

[2] See Whitehead, *Science and the Modern World,* p. 126-127.

but the universal is reached. In this context, a fact is concrete only if it is nonlocal or nondepartmental, while an abstraction is always partial or limited in its scope. To complete abstractions by appealing to concrete fact means to place partial truth(s) in the context of total truth. Accordingly, Whitehead is concerned with testimony from every quarter—from poets, prophets, statesmen, scientists, and all the rest.

Whitehead seems nowhere to develop any other interpretation of "concrete." Yet, we do not ordinarily regard things as nonlocal or nondepartmental unless they be concepts, and by comparison with that to which they refer, concepts are ordinarily thought to be abstract. This is why it strikes us as odd to speak of concrete conceptualization or of a concrete philosophical scheme of ideas. There can be no objection to using "concrete" as Whitehead does as long as we do not lose sight of the truth intended in the ordinary use of the term, namely, that words and concepts never exhaust the facts to which they refer. When we said above that philosophy is by nature abstract (in the ordinary but non-Whiteadian sense of "abstract"), our intention was to stress the gap between thought and things-thought-about. It would be going too far to claim that Whitehead does not acknowledge this gap.[3] But he makes little or nothing of it and instead concentrates on the gap between partial and complete knowledge. Because of the importance of the fact that no entity "in its depth" can be thought, Whitehead's doctrine that "a philosophic system should present an elucidation of concrete fact"[4] comes as a shock and a puzzle, at least on first reading. The key here is to recognize that Whitehead is using "concrete" in a special sense and is not denying the inalienable uniqueness of each particular entity.

It is obvious that any actual occasion enjoys a privacy of feeling and decision, a privacy no thought can ever penetrate.

---

[3]He seems almost to deny the gap when he asserts that he can discern no reason "why any factor in the universe should not be manifest in some flash of human consciousness." Whitehead, *Science and Philosophy,* p. 134.

[4]Whitehead, *Adventures of Ideas,* p. 187.

In ordinary parlance, we would say that such privacy of feeling and decision is the occasion in its concreteness. If philosophy cannot capture the occasion in its privacy of feeling and decision, can we assume that (in its full particularity) it is accessible at all? Here we face the epistemological question head-on. For process philosophy, the answer must be given in terms of prehension, each occasion being a datum destined to be prehended (felt) by occasions in its future and thereby immortalized. But as Whitehead says, "The present fact has not the past fact with it in any full immediacy."[5] Only in God is an occasion preserved without loss.

Certainly this doctrine is not free of difficulty, for how can God share the experience of a creature—a minor fragment of reality? He can, of course, experience a creature as one among the totality of creatures, that is, as part of his all-experience. But *this* creature, here and now, would not be a part—one among many—if it did not (at least to some extent) exclude other creatures. Indeed, its exclusions are essential to its distinctiveness. Without them, it would have no perspective on its actual world and hence no "place" in reality. God, because he is nonexclusive, cannot share the creature's perspective—in short, he cannot share its particularity. Hartshorne argues that God, though he is all-inclusive, is not guilty of the sins of men, since sin is deliberate exclusion of the interests of others, and God, precisely because he *is* all-inclusive, lacks any such exclusiveness. But, as we can see, the same logic applies to a creature's being the particular entity that it is, for, if God fails to share the entity's particularizing exclusions, he cannot share its particularity—any more than he can share its sin if he fails to share its sinful exclusions. Perhaps an illustration will help. You or I, though we are aware of our bodies, are not aware of what it would mean to *be* one of our big toes, much less a cell or occasion in that toe. This would be true even if our awareness of our bodies were maximally distinct, for a whole

---

[5]Whitehead, *Process and Reality,* p. 517.

cannot become or assume one of its own parts, no matter how much sympathy it has with that part.

It is necessary to put the point in a temporal context. For, after all, the divine whole of which an occasion is supposedly part is temporally posterior to that occasion—or to put it in simpler terms, the occasion is preserved in God's memory. Our question is whether the occasion can be preserved in God's memory *without loss.* God is not aware of the occasion when it is in process of self-formation—prehending its data, deciding its form of self-completion, enjoying its moment of satisfaction— simply because, as Whitehead says, no contemporary prehends another. Since prehension is the relation of present to past, it seems impossible for God ever to know an occasion "as it knew itself," to know it, that is, as a subject in its living immediacy, in its presentness of feeling and decision. He could not share the world of the occasion *without ceasing to be temporally posterior to it,* since the occasion, when it was present fact, faced an open future. Of course, if God ceased to be temporally posterior to the occasion, he would not be remembering it at all. We may put the point as follows. Since it is essential to the distinctiveness of an occasion to be itself and no other, its distinctiveness necessarily excludes its existing later (or earlier) than it does. Hence, God cannot, by prehending the occasion, share its distinctiveness, since in order to prehend it he must be temporally posterior to it. All this added up means that even for God there is loss—loss of full particularity—in the time stream. In order to make the argument more vivid, imagine God's remembering an occasion some distance in the past, say a young man's anticipation of being married in July, 1954. Aside from the question as to whether the anticipation of marriage is an experience that is open to God, there is the question as to whether it is possible for God to retain that particular instance of anticipation just as it was when present. Is God even now anticipating an event of 1954? If not, how has he preserved that occasion of anticipation? Yet, how could he possibly anticipate something he knows as already settled in all its details?

127

If our analysis is correct, we may conclude that there are depths in any actuality which no knowledge can plumb. This conclusion may seem to undercut the commonsense supposition that there is imperishable truth about any actuality at all, whether we know it or not. As we have seen, Hartshorne argues that this supposition presupposes the immortality of the past. But we are obliged to accept his argument only if it can be shown that an actuality is nothing *more* than the truth about it. This is exactly what our analysis has put in doubt, for if an actuality in its fullness transcends even divine knowledge, the truth about it fails to exhaust it. This is not to deny that there can be truth about an actuality only if it is *in some sense* preserved. An actuality may be inaccessible in one respect but not in all—and in these latter respects it is surely known and preserved by God.

All this raises the serious question: is God really all-inclusive? Hartshorne himself says that since each occasion is to some extent autonomous, God is not omnipotent in the sense of possessing absolutely all power. If God does not decide or enact our decisions, then they are not his, and he does not include us in the concreteness of our decision-making (although he may very well know about our decisions and forever remember them as facts). At one point Whitehead remarks: "It is as true to say that God transcends the World, as that the World transcends God."[6] The world's transcendence of God—like his transcendence of it—is inseparable from the mystery of individual selfhood and freedom.

To hold that the world transcends God makes it difficult to maintain that God is all-inclusive; but such transcendence is required for an understanding of sin and waywardness. There are many reasons why the doctrine of sin plays a relatively minor role in process philosophy. Doubtless the chief reason is that process philosophy is a metaphysical system, not a doctrine of man. But perhaps the intimacy of the world's relation to

---

[6]*Ibid.,* p. 528.

God and of God's relation to the world—a doctrine stressed in Hartshorne's thought—weighs against the development of a theory of radical estrangement from God. Such estrangement is possible only in the case of a significant (if limited) measure of freedom, a measure which would qualify the extent to which God creates the creature and, as we have tried to show, the extent to which he saves (preserves) it. Of course, Hartshorne affirms that creatures possess freedom and that at least human creatures sin. But the question is whether this affirmation entirely accords with the thesis that all things are internal to God and he to all things, and whether greater attention to the fact of human sin would not reveal serious lack of accord with that thesis.

In one respect, Whiteheadian thought precludes the possibility of failing to "do the good." For while an occasion can, according to its own decisions, synthesize its data in this way or that, it cannot fall short of aesthetic synthesis of some sort. This is simply the metaphysical situation. Since for Whitehead the basic form of value is the aesthetic, no occasion can fail to achieve value. Indeed, an occasion cannot even *intend* anything else, nonachievement of aesthetic synthesis being an impossibility. In short, the continuous realization of value, occasion by occasion, is a necessity. One may take exception to this doctrine and assert that value is something that *may or may not* be attained, not something to which there is no alternative at all. In addition, he may argue that at least for human beings, freedom unquestionably involves possibilities of evil, possibilities that upset the neatness and assembly-line regularity of Whitehead's picture. Of course, it may be that evil (like consciousness) represents a complication or special form of the simple, basic facts of reality and therefore has no place in a metaphysical description. But one wonders. Is evil at the human level merely a complication or special form of the process of aesthetic synthesis? Is it not rather an exception to that process?

At this point the reader may be asking himself: "Where do these criticisms leave process thought anyway?" In response, we offer two observations. First, these criticisms need to be evaluated. There is no reason to suppose that they are entirely cogent or unanswerable, or that they compel us to abandon process thought. "Our little systems" are never flawless; they should be criticized. But we must remember that criticism may represent failure to understand another's point of view and in any case may be far from decisive. Second, a position is strengthened to the extent that it can absorb or withstand criticism. Hartshorne remarks that one of the obstacles he has had to face in attempting to make his thought rationally solid is the dearth of careful criticism of his writing. "Objectivity," he adds, "is not in the individual thinker but in the process of mutual correction and inspiration."[7] Incidentally, it would be remiss of me to permit the reader to think that my own enthusiasm for process thought, scarcely concealed in the previous pages, has been dimmed by the criticisms put forth above.

What we have just said about the contribution that criticism can make to a position suggests that in order to do justice to process thought we are obliged to subject it to a more thorough-going and searching criticism than we have been able to offer here. (Obviously, such a criticism should be undertaken only after a sustained effort to understand process thought in all its intricacy.) Our discussion has revealed that two topics are especially pressing: the mystery and hiddenness of the concrete, and the nature and gravity of sin. Of course, there are many other topics which demand attention. All of these must be carefully considered by process philosophers and theologians, and answers must be developed and defended.

It may be that process thought can with profit be brought into relation with other systems of philosophy. Ogden says that "until process philosophy is informed by the insights of existential analysis, its lack of an explicit anthropology, which handicaps it for theological employment, can hardly be remedied in keeping with its own implicit principles."[8] Ogden is

---

[7] Hartshorne, *The Logic of Perfection*, p. ix.
[8] Ogden, *Christ Without Myth*, p. 152. Used by permission.

here suggesting that the doctrine of man which properly belongs to process philosophy (according to its own implicit principles) has been given expression by existentialist philosophers. It is not easy to believe that existentialism and process philosophy, like two lovers, were just made for one another. But even if the romance between the two were a bit turbulent and a marriage could not quite be brought off, much could be gained on both sides. To bring process philosophy into relation with existentialism would, for example, put it into juxtaposition with the thought of theologians like Rudolf Bultmann, who draw heavily on existential analysis and (at least from Ogden's point of view) need to develop the kind of full-orbed philosophical system represented by process philosophy.

Whatever becomes of the attempt to relate process philosophy and existentialism, it is increasingly evident that theologians are once more ready for dialogue with philosophers. The climate of opinion sometimes changes rapidly in the theological world. Continental Europe has been dominated since the 1920's by Karl Barth, whose coldness toward philosophy is notorious. But Barth has been succeeded in his teaching post at Basel by a young theologian named Heinrich Ott, who makes sympathetic use of the ontology of philosopher Martin Heidegger. Is this not a sign of rapprochement between "Jerusalem and Athens," a sign of the thawing and cracking of the old barriers between theology and philosophy? If so, it is vital that process theologians *make themselves heard* in theology, lest theologians continue to harbor many of the same old illusions about philosophy. Says Hartshorne:

A great deal of the discussion of metaphysics and philosophy of religion in our time has been rendered idle by the assumption that if "metaphysics" . . . were possible it would have to be the sort of thing which Hume and Kant knew and criticized, or perhaps Kant's own queer and truncated sort of metaphysics, or else the Absolute Idealism of the last century.[9]

------
[9]Hartshorne, *The Logic of Perfection*, p. ix. Used by permission.

Comment by Professor Charles Hartshorne

THIS COMMENT UPON A BOOK which I cordially recommend as a readable and helpful introduction to an important type of philosophy will be somewhat personal.

That natural science, physics, biology, astronomy have a new vision of reality, worked out during the past hundred years or so, is rather widely known to even slightly educated people. But that speculative philosophy or metaphysics has during the same period arrived at new perspectives is not widely known. It is true nevertheless. These new perspectives are not the single-handed creation of any one man. Bergson in one way, C. S. Peirce in another, James Ward in another, Nicolas Berdyaev in another, the Italian mathematician and philosopher Varisco in another, E. S. Brightman in another, my teacher, W. E. Hocking, in another, the pre-Whiteheadian Charles Hartshorne in another, might all be called process philosophers. And the list is still far from complete. Before any of those mentioned came Fechner, the great German scientist and natural theologian; Jules Lequier, brilliant, tragic, unfortunately neglected French philosopher; and the German theologian Pfleiderer. Before them came Schelling, in his little-known last phase, and long before him Fausto Sozzini and his followers. Common to these men was the rejection of the supposed axiom of theology for two thousand years: "God" stands for a being in all respects immutable, complete, self-sufficient, or absolute. Rather they all believed that God is both immutable and mutable, both self-sufficient and derivative from his creation, and that there is no

133

contradiction in this, since the immutable and mutable, self-sufficient and derivative, apply to different aspects of the divine life. My own arrival at this view seems to have been most definitely due to Hocking, certainly not to Whitehead, who merely confirmed it. Probably Bergson and Brightman also influenced me. I seem to recall having virtually reached the view at a time when the only philosophers I had read were Royce *(Problem of Christianity)*, William James *(Varieties of Religious Experience)*, and Emerson *(Essays)*—in none of which the idea is to be found. It is really a natural enough conception if one has not been drilled from an early age in the more usual view. It is quite possible that my early teacher, Rufus Jones, in whose course on the history of Christian doctrine (1916) I had read Royce, had introduced me to the conception. The point is, this way of thinking is a product of the age, not of any single genius. Whereas from Aristotle to Kant almost no one thought of admitting an aspect of change and relativity (including contingency) in God himself, during the past twelve decades or more this admission has been more and more widely and boldly proposed. Of course, some have even gone so far as to question whether there be anything eternally the same in Deity, any aspect of independence or absoluteness. J. S. Mill, S. Alexander, and William James are examples of this extreme tendency. I was for a short time somewhat under James's spell, but it is 45 years since this notion of a *merely* finite God has had any attraction for me.

If even Deity is in process, of course his creatures must be, for God is the supreme form, while his creatures are instances of nonsupreme forms, of the universal traits of reality. (I cannot clearly recall ever having thought of God as mere exception to the universal categories, though, of course, long ago I became aware that many have done so.)

If there are any processes at all, experiencing is a process. So the question is, are there two kinds of process, experiencing and something else, say merely material process? This issue was decided for me by much rather solitary reflection when I was a private in a comparatively quiet base hospital in France during World War I. I saw, as I thought, the vacuousness of the notion of "merely material" processes. The only philosopher I recall having previously read on the question was Emerson, years before. Probably his subjective idealism is the first source of my rather different "panpsychism" or, as I prefer now to call it, "psychicalism." The conviction was confirmed by my teacher in psychology, L. T. Troland, and many other influences. But mainly I thought, and still think, that reflection upon experience, if sufficiently attentive, careful, and dispassionate, will convince anyone (a) that an ultimate dualism of mind and mere matter is an absurdity, and (b) that a monism of mere matter is only the same dualism in disguise, since no one can effectively think that there is no such thing as thinking (or know by experience that there is no such thing as experience) while he perfectly well can think that there is no such thing as mere matter, wholly devoid of feeling or awareness. Moreover, sensory experience, the source of our empirical knowledge, does not exhibit mere "dead matter," as I tried to prove in my book *The Philosophy and Psychology of Sensation*. As he told me once, Whitehead reached his form of psychicalism by a similar route.

The universality of process and of experiencing as traits of reality are not enough to characterize "process philosophy." An essential idea is the equally general role of what Whitehead calls "creativity." Not just God creates, but his creatures do also. Moreover, in both cases creation is first of all self-creation, and only derivatively production of individually distinct beings. A century before Whitehead, Lequier had said, "God has created me creator of myself." Why did he say this? For reasons somewhat similar to those which led me about 1921 (though I knew nothing of Lequier and next to nothing of Whitehead) to say it in a student essay called "The Self Its Own Maker." Lequier's reason was this: we say we "make our own decisions." True, we also say that God has made us. Has he even made our decisions? How, then, are they ours rather than his? And what is a person apart from the sum of his past decisions? If I make my decisions, then to some extent I make myself. And therefore, if I do not to some extent make myself, when I say I make decisions or decide, I am talking nonsense. Further, if decision making is nothing in me, then when I speak of God deciding this or that (e.g., issuing a fiat, *Let there be light*), I use words without meaning in my experience. Lequier saw, as few had seen before him (the Socinians being about the only exceptions), the illegitimacy of trying to take "freedom" seriously in application to God while explaining it away in application to man. I can talk about divine freedom or creativity only because I am genuinely free myself. And freedom means making one's own character, this being a sort of deposit of past uses of one's freedom. Thus when Whitehead and the French writer Sartre independently speak of man as *"causa sui,"* self-caused, they are a century later duplicating Lequier's reasoning.

Lequier saw something else. If I make something in myself, I also make something in all who know me. Deciding to be the person who has done *this* when he might have been the person who has done *that* is deciding that one's acquaintances will henceforth have the one person to know, not the other. *This* (that is, the latter) person will never be known as an existent; for it will never exist. Above all, God will know that I have become the person I have made myself to be, not the person I now will never be since I decided not to be that person. Thus freedom means not only self-creation but creation of features in the knowledge of all by whom one is known, especially in the knowledge of God who alone cannot fail to know all as they are. With this step we are close to Whitehead's idea of God. Somewhat similar remarks could be made about Fechner as about Lequier. Both imply a real distinction in God between what he always is and what he becomes in consequence of free decisions in the creatures.

136

We have still not arrived at process philosophy in the full sense. One must generalize the foregoing reasoning for all creatures, creatures as such. God has divine self-creativity (productive of reality in others), human beings have the human form of self-creativity, dogs have the doggish form, amoebae the amoebic form, atoms the atomic form. There is no logic in restricting creative power to God and man. It is as though one were to say, there are two numerical ideas, infinity, and a certain range of finite numbers, *n* down to *m,* below which is simply zero. Human freedom may be slight compared to the divine, but even so, to suppose that there is no room between it and absolute unfreedom is wholly arbitrary. Between any number, however small, and zero an infinity of fractions can be put. Leibniz used this argument in favor of his form of psychicalism. God has supreme awareness, the creatures lesser forms of awareness, each kind of creature its own form. (This valuable contribution to metaphysics goes back to Campanella, Telesio, and other Renaissance thinkers.) The same reasoning, as Leibniz failed to see, should apply to creative power. Lequier perhaps did not quite take this step. But he did say freedom should be *the* ultimate philosophical conception, and this implies the possibility of the generalization in question. Fechner, here too, is similar and somewhat more explicit. Schelling had some such notion, partly hidden in his cloudy post-Kantian dialectic.

The foregoing ideas are all at least hinted at in the writings of Peirce, which I began to study intensively just at the time I also began to study Whitehead intensively. I can scarcely imagine my subsequent philosophical development without that exposure to Peirce. But Peirce was confused and confusing in what he said about God. Here I learned little from him.

There was another confusion in Peirce. He could not come to any clear view of the relations of continuity and discontinuity in process—which for him, as for other psychicalists, was the same as experiencing in some form, human or nonhuman. It is precisely at this point that Whitehead, in my opinion, made his greatest contribution to process philosophy. All the other philosophers I have mentioned above talk as though experiencing were a continuous affair. But in a true continuum there are no definite unitary parts. "How many experiences does one have between awakening in the morning and going into a dreamless sleep at night?" To this question those who assume a sheer continuum of experiencing must answer, "An infinite number." Nay, they must say that as many experiences occur in the first minute of the day as in the entire day. Other paradoxes also arise. Zeno long before, with great genius, realized that the notion of "many realities" makes sense only if one can justify the idea that the geometrical continuum, with its endless divisibility, is not legislative for concrete actuality. Zeno argued that it must be so legislative and that consequently, pluralism, the assertion of many realities, is untenable. William James, before Whitehead, had the courage to face the issue squarely and assert the discontinuity of experiencing. Whitehead agreed with him. Without Whitehead I should still have been a process philosopher, but probably one unable to extricate himself from the Zeno paradoxes. Peirce was prequantum-mechanics, but worse than that, he was explicitly antiquantum. He raised the issue and (except for one confession of uncertainty) decided it in favor of continuity. Whitehead was presumably helped by quantum physics to make the other decision. But no matter what physics might say, purely philosophically, I hold that Peirce was wrong and Whitehead was right. Whitehead is, so far as I know, the sole great speculative philosopher in the West (apart from some little-known Mohammedan philosophers of many centuries ago) to give a solution of the Zeno problem which really saves pluralism, and to weave the doctrine of quanta of becoming so thoroughly into all his other doctrines—with one exception—that one can say, Never for one moment does he, in his Harvard or metaphysical phase, forget that concrete processes occur one by one, and not as endlessly divisible portions of a continuum. The Buddhists, a thousand years before, had held this doctrine, which Whitehead, I presume, arrived at independently.

The "exception" is the idea of God. And here is one point at which Whitehead and I differ rather sharply. He says God is the supreme form of "actual entity"; my view is, he is the supreme form of the category of "personally ordered society" of actual entities. Technically this difference is important. In thinking about God, Whitehead, it seems to me, fell into the trap which held Peirce to some extent enchained, the trap of taking continuity to apply literally to actuality. For Whitehead's God changes, while an actual entity, though it "becomes," does not change. Hence God must be a series, or society, of actual entities. Only societies can change.

I also have reservations about Whitehead's "eternal objects." Nominalistic or anti-Platonic arguments impress me more than they did Whitehead. And here I get help from Peirce. Actuality is "incurably atomic" or discrete, says Whitehead, and rightly so. But possibility, in its pure or eternal form, is, as Peirce insists and Whitehead seems at times to forget, essentially continuous. Hence it is misleading to talk of "eternal objects" as though this were a definite plurality. It is a continuous matrix out of which all plurality is created. But this hint must here suffice.

In most respects I do accept Whitehead's theory of reality. But experience has shown that his exposition of this theory, and his defense of it against possible objections, are for many philosophers quite unconvincing, inadequate, and even repellent. This is why I have felt called upon to function to a certain extent as an "advocate," in Dr. Peters' phrase. It has seemed very clear to me that most of his contemporaries were, for one reason or another, incapable of finding in Whitehead much of importance that is actually there. My differences from Whitehead are thus more procedural or methodological than substantive. Among these procedural differences is the following.

I think one cannot meet current skepticism, positivism, and linguistic analysis without more careful or explicit discussion than Whitehead gives of the difference between empirical science and pure metaphysics, also of the relation between metaphysics and formal (also "informal") logic. A key to the logical nature of metaphysics in general, and particularly the metaphysics of religion, I find in the ontological argument for God's existence. My *Anselm's Discovery* deals with systematic and historical aspects of this topic, which is, though less extensively, discussed in most of my other books. Whitehead said almost nothing about this. It has always been methodologically quite central for me. Here we have almost an entire dimension lacking in his approach, and yet a dimension he would, I believe, have seen the point of developing. There are certain other dimensions with which I hope to deal in a systematic work on metaphysics. Process philosophy is not yet in a form by which it must stand or fall. There are resources of argument and analysis which must be drawn upon before that can be said.

It remains only to say something about Dr. Peters' admirable study. I find his exposition lucid, interesting, and accurate. I am attracted also by his application of the philosophical ideas to the question of the incarnation.

In reply to his critical final chapter in which he finds difficulty, modestly conceding it may not be valid or conclusive, in the idea that God fully knows our limited states of mind without being similarly limited, I will confess that I do not find the difficulty more than a subtle one of words. God "participates in our limited experiences without incurring their limitations" means that he experiences all the quality of those experiences, including any qualitative contribution of enjoyment or suffering the limitations make to them, but yet is not himself likewise limited. Is this really a contradiction? Suppose, after discovering the answer to a certain question, I recall how I felt when wondering what the answer was, does it follow that I still do not know the answer? I remember what it felt like not to know it, but I can distinguish this from my present feeling, now that I do know the answer.

I suggest, as a counterargument to Dr. Peters' objection, the following. If to know more is *ipso facto* to fail to know what it is like to know less, then being wise means a proportional inability to understand folly, and the struggle for wisdom is a struggle to be less and less able to understand the majority of mankind or one's own past. In other words, if the objection proved anything it would "prove too much," and thereby its lack of soundness is shown. Let us take the example of our awareness of our own bodily cells. It is said that even were this awareness wholly distinct it would not enable us to know the cells in their particularity, since this depends upon their limitations, which cannot be ours. But all I get from this is that were the awareness distinct it would be indistinct. In the visual field each bit of color is a limited part of the field. I am not thus limited, for I have the entire field in my awareness. Does it follow that I am not aware of the limitation, the partiality, of each color bit? On the contrary, whereas for the bit, were it aware, the limitation might be a vague sense of a beyond, for me it is the definite failure of the bits to encompass the whole field, and it is this for me just because I do not myself fail in that same sense. Even the vague sense of a beyond could be an item in my awareness, as when I have in mind how vaguely I looked forward to a career in philosophy when, as a student, I made the decision to undertake such a career. I now know what the career has been like, but also, so far as my memory extends to that early time, what it was like not to know this.

Concerning sin, the difficulty of understanding human motivation does not seem to me to arise from the idea that my feelings are precisely and fully included in the divine consciousness. It is rather something like the old Socratic mystery, how can one know the good and not want to actualize it? Or, if one does not know the good which one fails to act upon, the failure must be innocent. The idea of God's being fully aware of the good, and of my state, does not produce this paradox, which turns upon what we know, not what God knows. Whitehead hints (*Adventures of Ideas,* chapter on Peace) at something like Reinhold Niebuhr's theory that sin is essentially the religious vision gone wrong. Man, being aware of God sufficiently to realize that he himself is not the center and goal of existence, but not sufficiently to be reconciled to this situation, rebels and tries to make himself that center after all. He tries to be God. The other animals just are the center, for themselves, and innocently so. It is very likely true that much more needs to be said than has been said on this subject by the philosophers mentioned in this book, but the topic is difficult. Man is almost too close to himself to be able to think honestly about himself. And, in so far as sin is historical, a contingent fact about the human species, it is of course outside metaphysics as such, and belongs to anthropology, psychology, or theology. I cannot see how it would help to suppose that even God does not adequately include in his consciousness what goes on in us.

Dr. Peters is not the only one to be troubled by the apparent paradox of the infallible knower understanding what it is to be fallible, the deathless one understanding what it is to be afraid of death, etc., just as, conversely, many have found themselves unable to believe that we fallible and mortal beings can form any genuine conception at all of infallibility or eternity. But I think that if either paradox were really genuine, it is not to be understood how the question could ever even have arisen. We understand basic concepts by contrast, fallibility by infallibility, and vice versa. Man could not escape from the innocence of the other animals were he not able somehow to think God, and therewith rise in some fashion above the partialities of his animal mode of perceiving reality. But in having the divine or impartial point of view he also does not have it; while God simply has it. Somehow, out of this having and not having, temptation arises. Would it really help to suppose that even God does not grasp reality as it is?

I know a fine German student of Whitehead (taught by me) who feels the same difficulty as Dr. Peters. Somehow, though, I do not find it very troublesome. I wish I could say this for every difficulty which can be brought forward! Alas, human instruments, including human philosophical systems, never do all that one might wish them to do as smoothly and perfectly as one might wish them to do it. With this understatement, and with heartfelt thanks to my good friend, I close this comment.

CHARLES HARTSHORNE

The University of Texas

Appendix

THE READER who wishes to begin reading Whitehead might first look into the essays in Part I of *Science and Philosophy*. This section of the book contains personal and autobiographical reflections. Of course, the reader will find essays in the remainder of the volume readable and illuminating. As a next step, he might read Part III of *Modes of Thought*, where he will find a general, nontechnical presentation of Whitehead's doctrine of the unity of nature and life. The reader is advised to read next the first six chapters of *Science and the Modern World*, which constitute a critical and historical treatment of modern science and its underlying philosophical assumptions. To get into Whitehead's system, the reader will have to turn to something more difficult and technical, for example, to the chapters in the remainder of *Science and the Modern World*. Many find Parts III and IV of *Adventures of Ideas* the most rewarding exposition of the philosophy of organism. The beginner might with profit tackle the first and even the final two chapters of *Process and Reality*, but he is likely to be mystified by the remainder of the volume (a full but highly technical presentation of Whitehead's mature philosophical thought, the classic statement of process metaphysics). The following, shorter works of Whitehead each deal with a special topic, and the Whitehead beginner who is a diligent reader should be able to manage several of them: *Religion in the Making; Symbolism: Its Meaning and Effect; The Aims of Education;* and *The Function of Reason*.

A complete bibliography of the philosophical works of Whitehead can be found in *The Philosophy of Alfred North Whitehead,* ed. Paul Arthur Schilpp (New York: Tudor Publishing Company, 1951).

The following is a chronological listing of the books suggested above, with publication data.

Whitehead, Alfred North. *Science and the Modern World.* New York: The Macmillan Company, 1925. Paperback edition: MT 551—Mentor Books (New American Library of World Literature, Inc.).

_____. *Religion in the Making.* New York: The Macmillan Company, 1926. Paperback edition: LA 28—Meridian Books (The World Publishing Co.).

_____. *Symbolism: Its Meaning and Effect.* New York: The Macmillan Company, 1927. Paperback edition: 13—Capricorn Books (C. P. Putnam's Sons).

_____. *Process and Reality.* New York: The Macmillan Company, 1929. Paperback edition: TB 1033—Harper Torchbooks (Harper and Row, Publishers).

_____. *The Function of Reason.* Princeton: Princeton University Press, 1929. Paperback edition: BP 72—Beacon Press.

_____. *The Aims of Education.* New York: The Macmillan Company, 1929. Paperback edition: MP 373—Mentor Books (New American Library of World Literature, Inc.).

_____. *Adventures of Ideas.* New York: The Macmillan Company, 1933. Paperback edition: MT 551—Mentor Books (New American Library of World Literature, Inc.).

——————————————. *Modes of Thought*. New York: The Macmillan Company, 1938. Paperback edition: 5— Capricorn Books (C. P. Putnam's Sons).

——————————————. *Science and Philosophy*. New York: Philosophical Library, Inc., 1948. Paperback edition: 12—Wisdom Library Paperbacks (Philosophical Library, Inc.).

One of the best places to begin the study of Hartshorne is with his little book, *The Divine Relativity*, a concise and illuminating presentation of the social conception of Deity. The reader will perhaps wish to follow up with *Man's Vision of God*, a more extensive and detailed treatment of the social conception of Deity, with attention to the logic of theism. Both books, long out of print, have been reissued. *Reality as Social Process* is a collection of essays dealing with a variety of topics in philosophy and religion. It is not highly technical, and most of it can be read profitably by the average reader. Far more difficult is *The Logic of Perfection*, a recent work. The book consists of a number of essays, of which the longest and by far the most important is "Ten Ontological or Modal Proofs for God's Existence" (Chapter II). The reader may find *Philosophers Speak of God* of interest. It is a work in which Hartshorne, in collaboration with William L. Reese, provides introductory as well as critical commentary on a variety of passages with theological import, selected from the entire history of thought, chiefly from philosophical writings. Unfortunately, Hartshorne's two earliest books, *The Philosophy and Psychology of Sensation*[1] and *Beyond Humanism,* are at present out of print. However, copies (at least of the latter book) are available in many libraries across the country. *Anselm's Discovery* was pub-

---

[1]Copies of *The Philosophy and Psychology of Sensation* may be secured by addressing Mrs. Charles Hartshorne, 724 Sparks Avenue, Austin, Texas 78705.

lished in 1965. In this volume Hartshorne deals extensively with the ontological argument for divine existence, presenting and discussing the views of numerous philosophers and theologians on the topic. In addition, *A Natural Theology for Our Times* is to be published in 1967. It contains the three lectures on natural theology that Hartshorne delivered at Union Seminary, New York, in the fall of 1964.

The following is a chronological listing of the books suggested above, with publication data.

Hartshorne, Charles. *The Philosophy and Psychology of Sensation*. Chicago: The University of Chicago Press, 1934.

_____. *Beyond Humanism*. Chicago: Willett, Clark & Company, 1937.

_____. *Man's Vision of God*. Chicago: Willett, Clark & Company, 1941. Reissued (hardback) in 1964 as an Archon Book.

_____. *The Divine Relativity*. New Haven: Yale University Press, 1948. Paperback edition: Y 109—Yale University Press.

_____. *Reality as Social Process*. Glencoe, Ill.: The Free Press, 1953.

_____ (and William L. Reese). *Philosophers Speak of God*. Chicago: The University of Chicago Press, 1953. Paperback edition: P 142—Phoenix Books (The University of Chicago Press).

_____. *The Logic of Perfection*. La Salle, Ill.: Open Court Publishing Company, 1962. Paperback edition: P 85—The Open Court Publishing Company.

——————————. *Anselm's Discovery.* La Salle, Ill.: Open Court Publishing Company, 1965.

——————————. *A Natural Theology for Our Times.* La Salle, Ill.: Open Court Publishing Company. To be published in 1967.

To this list of works by Hartshorne may be added *Process and Divinity*, a *Festschrift* in his honor. Edited by William L. Reese and Eugene Freeman, it was published in 1964 by The Open Court Publishing Company of La Salle, Illinois.

Index

149

GURDJIEFF

THREE LECTURES

GURDJIEFF

A Very Great Enigma

THREE LECTURES

by

J. G. Bennett

DISCARD

Given at Denison House,
Summer, 1963

SAMUEL WEISER
New York
1973

Published by
SAMUEL WEISER, INC.
734 Broadway
New York, New York 10003

ISBN 0-87728-216-1

Library of Congress Catalogue Card No. 72-91951

Printed in U.S.A. by
NOBLE OFFSET PRINTERS, INC.
New York, N.Y. 10003

Lecture I

GURDJIEFF'S BACKGROUND   1

The Greeks of Caesaria, Alexandropol and Kars--the
cockpit of the Caucasus. Early Invasions, Turks,
Armenians, Greeks, Assyrians, Dukhobor, Molokans
and Yezidis. The Sack of Kars, April 24, 1877.
The incredible environment of Gurdjieff's boyhood.

Lecture II

THE SOURCES OF GURDJIEFF'S IDEAS   30

The Eastern Churches, Armenian Secret Societies,
Sufism and the Dervish Brotherhoods, Sufi Recluses
of Persia and Turkestan. The 'People of Truth.'
Gurdjieff as a Professional Wonder Worker. Russian
Occultism. The Source of the Enneagram. Babylon
and Zoroastrian influences in Gurdjieff's Ideas.

Lecture III

GURDJIEFF'S TEACHING AND METHODS   70

Stages of Development from 1889-1949. The Way of
Malamat and its significance for understanding his
life. The Basic Human Problems. Gurdjieff's Practical Methods. Is there anything wholly new in
Gurdjieff's Cosmology? Precursors of the New Epoch.
The Final Enigma. How did Gurdjieff intend his
work to continue?

GURDJIEFF'S BACKGROUND

Gurdjieff was a very great enigma in more ways than one. First and most obvious is the fact that no two people who knew him would agree as to who and what he was. If you look at the various books that have been written about Gurdjieff and if you look at his own writings, you will find that no two pictures are the same. Everyone who knew him, upon reading what other people have written about him, feels that they have not got it right. Each one of us believes we saw something that other people did not see. This is no doubt true. It went with the peculiar habit he had of hiding himself, of appearing to be something other than he really was. This was very confusing, and it began from the time he was first known in European countries.

Another enigma connected with Gurdjieff, concerns the sources of his teaching and methods. He never openly disclosed where he himself had learned. Anyone who takes the trouble to examine his teaching and his methods, can assign nearly every fragment to some known tradition. We can say that this theme came from the Greek Orthodox

1

tradition, that theme came from an Assyrian or Babylonian tradition, another was clearly Muslim and connected with Sufism and even with this or that particular Sufi sect. One can say of others that they must have come from one or other of the branches of Buddhism. Again, there are indications that he took much from what is called the Western occult tradition, the Platonic and Rosicrucian tradition. But when one examines still more closely, we find that there is something that cannot be assigned to any known traditions. There are certain very important features of which one cannot find any trace in literature. I will have more to say about these in the next lecture.

If Gurdjieff were no more than a syncretist, a reformer who put together fragments from various well-known traditions or even secret traditions that he managed to unearth in the course of his search; then he would occupy one place. If, on the other hand, there is something wholly original, which cannot be referred back to any earlier known or secret tradition, then he occupies quite a different place. Herein lies the second enigma of Gurdjieff; which of these two places does he occupy? Was he just a clever man who was able to travel and search widely, to discover many things, to read a great deal, having access to sources in many different languages, and out of all the material so collected, to construct something? Or, was he a man who, in addition to all that - because he certainly did all that - had some direct insight that was peculiarly his own, and that was both important and also not traceable to any earlier source? That would make him a man of special importance, because true innovators are very rare in the history of spiritual ideas.

There is a third enigma about which I am going to speak specially this evening because it struck me with great force, when I visited the scenes of Gurdjieff's early days a few weeks ago; and that is to explain how such a man could have come from such an environment. I saw, playing in the town of Kars in what used to be the old Greek Quarter, scores of little boys who ran after us wanting to be photographed and asking for bakshish: any one of whom might have been a young Gurdjieff. But the highest any of those boys can aspire to is probably to become a chauffeur, or possibly to get into the police - which is also a coveted profression.

The region between the Caucasus and Kurdistan is a very strange part of the world, and I must start by telling you a little about its geography and history. I had this map made, and it is an arrangement of the maps of this part of the world with which you are probably not familiar; as the usual maps either show Turkey in Asia, Russia, and Iran as separate units. In reality, this region is a coherent and well-defined geographical unit. (See end of this chapter for Map of Near East.) It is well-defined because it is dominated by the great mountains of

3

the Caucasus and Kurdistan, with Mount Ararat here, the highest mountain after you leave the great central Asian massif right away until you come to the Mediterranean. Ararat is higher than any of the mountains of the Alps. These great mountain areas cover a greater surface than the Alps. Most of the area on this map is more than 3,000 feet above sea level, and the highest mountains go up to 15,000 feet and more. There is a great natural barrier that separates Europe and Asia. It runs from the Urals in the North, through the Caspian Sea to the great masses of the Caucasus and Kurdistan shown on the map. This barrier has checked the migrations of populations east and west except through a few narrow channels. The most important of these channels runs northwest from Tabriz to Kars and then almost due west through Erzerum where it joins the valley of the Euphrates River. To the east of Erzerum is a watershed at a height of about 7,000 feet above sea level; but the pass can easily be negotiated in summer.

From time immemorial, and by that I mean a good 10,000 years, people have passed through that route. After the ending of the Ice Ages, when people began to travel southward and occupy these regions; this was one of the great migration routes. Wave after wave of invasion has entered that way: Parthians, Karduks and Armenians, Tartars, Mongols, and Turks. Genghis Khan and Tamerlane and other famous conquerors followed this route. The Seljuks and Ottoman Turks between the 10th and 15th centuries established Islam in Asia Minor by the way of the Caucasus route. Each wave of invasion was resisted, and one of the natural places of defence against invaders was a natural fortress that for many centuries has been known as the Fortress of Kars. When one stands upon Kars fortress, built on a rock dominating a narrow valley, one sees mountains in every direction, covered with snow at all times in the year. Kars has been besieged, defended and taken, again and again. At one time, it has been not Kars itself but the nearby city of Ani, which was the capital of the Bagratian Armenian kingdom of the 8th and 10th centuries. This region has been the place where invasions have been thwarted, turned back, resumed and finally broken through. Tamerlane himself twice tried unsuccessfully to break through this gap, and only did so when he brought up a second army, the first time he had to do so in all his conquests.

Not all movement came from the East. There were also invasions from Europe and Asia Minor: Greeks, Romans and Ottoman Turks and invasions from the North: Slavs and Caucasians. In the 19th century, this wave and counter-wave of invasion was resumed, this time between the Russian Empire and the Turkish Empire, in 1809, in 1814, 1855, and again in 1877 there were wars between Russia and Turkey, and always the main brunt of the fighting was taken somewhere here. The frontier between the two countries has always run a little to the East or a little to the West of this point.

Because it is near a frontier, Kars has never been regarded as a safe place. It has been built and destroyed and rebuilt and destroyed again. The town itself – as all these towns round here – is filled with mounds of rubble. I am sure that all this has had a powerful effect on the psyche of the people of this part of the world. They have lived for centuries, if not for thousands of years, in a state of stress, never knowing when an attack was going to come from the East or from the West. And undoubtedly Gurdjieff himself was subject to this stress. One of the worst experiences of the city of Kars was in October 1877, when it was taken by the Russians and there was terrible destruction at that time. I have looked at the history both from the Russian and the Turkish point of view. According to the Turks, there was just a wild massacre on the part of the Russians which lasted for three days. The Russian history says that the Turks resisted in a very foolish way and that pockets of resistance were gradually wiped out, but probably the two stories refer to the same event.

Before 1877, Kars was a considerable town. It had over 20,000 inhabitants and round it was relatively rich country. It is nothing like so rich as it gets lower towards Tabriz, but still fertile. Kars was taken by assault by the Russians in 1877, and in the following year, when the Russians had to give up what they had taken away up here in the Balkans, they were confirmed in the retention of Batoum, Kars and Ardahan. At that time, about 80 per cent of the population was Turkish. After the Russian conquest there was a great exodus and about 80,000 Turks migrated westwards in the next two or three years, and the Russians themselves brought non-Turks from all over this part of the world. They brought Greeks who themselves wanted to leave Turkey. Armenians were brought in from the South Caspian region. Assyrians - Aisors as they are called there - were brought up from Iraq. Quite a considerable number of Yezidis were persuaded to migrate to the North and settle in this part of the world. Heterodox sects such as the Molokans and Dukhobors came from Russia and even Esthonian Lutherans. So that between 1877 and the early 1880's, there was an extraordinary mix-up in this part of the world. Tens of thousands of families were moved hither and thither against their will.

You must understand that all this moving about was part of the policy of these governments. No one knew what to do with the disaffected populations. The Russians did not know what to do with the large Muslim population that was hostile to the Russian domination; the Turks did not know what to do with their large Christian population, which was equally hostile to them.

These were the conditions of Gurdjieff's boyhood. So far as I myself can make out from various
sources, from what he himself and his family have
told us, it does seem probable that he was born in
1872, in Alexandropol, and that his father moved to
Kars soon after it was taken by the Russians, that
is to say, somewhere about 1878, when he was six
or so years old.

I do not know if you can picture the state of
tension and distress that is caused by this kind of
situation. I myself was in Greece in 1925, when
there was the great exchange of populations. A mil-
lion and a half Greeks were taken out of Asia Minor
and dumped in Old Greece, and 400,000 Turks were
taken from Macedonia and Thrace and dumped in Asia
Minor. It was heartrending to see these unfortunate
people being sent to a country with different geographical conditions, different ways of life from their
own, with the jealousy of the population that was
being asked to receive them, the difficulty of getting
land for them to settle in. I expect that some of you
will have seen the even more distressing migrations
of Arabs in Jordan. You may have visited, as I have,
the refugee camps there, or have seen in Damascus
what happened to the unfortunate Kurds and Tartars
and others who were moved down from the Black Sea
coast. Only if you have seen it with your own eyes
can you get a picture of the distress that there is in
these forced movements of populations who do not
understand why they are being moved or where they

will end up.

Such things were happening in the Caucasus when Gurdjieff was a boy. He was only a child when the worst of it happened, and by the time he was six or seven years old, there is no doubt that things had begun to settle down. When his father moved to Kars, which had been reconstructed after the frightful destruction and carnage of October 1877, there was already some hope of peace and quiet.

There were other hardships to be borne, due to the severe climatic conditions. It is bitterly cold in the winter; it goes down to 30-40 degrees below freezing every winter and remains cold for several months, so that they have continual snow. There is a sudden thaw in the early spring, and about six weeks or two months of mud - which I can certify, having been there myself a couple months ago when you can hardly think of anything but the mud which surrounds you everywhere. Then comes the dry summer when all the mud turns to dust; and they have four or five months of intensely hot dry weather. These are not comfortable conditions of existence, especially for people who have got no satisfactory homes. At all times, as far as I can make out, the poorer population of Kars and of these other towns round about, have lived rather miserably in mud huts, sometimes under ground level, holes in the ground with roofs put over them and even a path going over the top of the roof. So that when you walk about, you sometimes do not know that you are walking on top of somebody's roof, until you see someone coming out below you.

These are the conditions as they are today. What it can have been like 80 or 90 years ago, I do not like to think. They must have been very bitter conditions. Gurdjieff in his own book, <u>Meetings with Remarkable Men</u>, does not to my mind really convey the sharpness of the conditions when he writes about his father and his first tutor. This is probably because he himself was so toughened by all the hardships that it did not seem to him anything special to write about. But I think you should have this picture of the severity of the conditions of existence, combined with the strain of war and the migration of populations, in order to picture to yourselves what a strange thing it is that out of all that a man could come who could make his mark on the world by intellectual power as well as psychic power that impressed so many hundreds of people, not themselves stupid, who came in contact with him.

You must look, however, at another side of this. That with this severity of physical and psychological conditions, also this part of the world is particularly richly endowed with traditional material. The population, when Gurdjieff was a boy, was, as I said, predominantly Muslim, and he learnt to talk Turkish from childhood. He talked Turkish, when I first knew him, better, I think, than he spoke Russian. Now the Turks, especially in the Eastern <u>vil-</u><u>ayete</u>, are very devoted to the mystical side of Islam, to Sufism. There always have been many Dervish communities in this part of the world. There is no question that Gurdjieff was influenced by Islamic mysticism, but at the same time he was also in a region of strong Greek and Russian Christian spirituality. Thirdly, he was himself half Armenian for his mother was an Armenian. That part of the world was really more Armenian than anything. The Armenians begin to preponderate as soon as you cross over the valley where present-day Armenia now is. The Armenians have quite separate traditions from either the Western or the Greek and Russian Orthodox Christians. There is the very ancient Armenian tradition of which Nakhichevan is the sacred city. This Armenian tradition is blended with other, older, pre-Christian traditions. Not only that, there are the Assyrians, the descendants of the Chaldeans, the Aisors as they are called there. Various communities still exist which have preserved traces of the ancient Babylonian, Zoroastrian and Mithraic mysteries and mysticism. The Yezidis are a special branch, with which Gurdjieff came into contact, with their own form of the Babylonian dualistic belief in the conflict of two powers in the world - the powers of good and evil, which is the basis of the Zoroastrian tradition.

Not only these comparatively well-known, but also many obscure sects, existed then and still do exist there today. I wonder whether there is anywhere else in the world where one can point to such a variety of influences that a young man touched by the need for spirituality could come in contact as here in this part of the Caucasus. It is close to Iran, where a strong Sufi tradition remained then and certainly still remains to this day. It is close to Armenia, close also to the quite different mystical traditions of the Turkish Sufis. In a way, therefore, one can say that together with all the influences that would make life very hard, there was also, to anyone who could feel for it, a very rich fund of traditional beliefs and practices in that very environment in which Gurdjieff was born. He gives some indications of all this in his own writings, in the <u>Meetings</u> <u>with</u> <u>Remarkable</u> <u>Men</u>, which probably most of you have read.

But between these two things, the very difficult conditions of life of a poor Greek-Armenian boy living in the Greek quarter of Kars, barely able to attend the newly built Russian town school; how could any reconciling understanding arise? How could he get a chance? One of the many strange events in the story of Gurdjieff is that he began to make contacts which could neither be ascribed to his own personal background, his parentage, his connection with the Greeks and Armenians, nor with the sort of influences that would be surrounding him in that Greek quarter - there were also, as I said, people from the Assyrians and Molokans and so on, but none of those - as I know from having seen in other parts of this world - had anything to give that could change Gurdjieff in the way he has been changed. He came in contact, while still a boy, with the Russian community, and by extraordinary good fortune, with the Russian community surrounding the Russian Orthodox Church in Kars, the Church that was established immediately after the conquest in 1877 for the Russian Army of occupation. Most of you will have read and it would be a waste of time for me to repeat the story of his contact with the Dean Borsh of the Military Cathedral and with other priests of the Cathedral, and how they taught him and of how he was able to develop some contact with the Western culture of his time.

Now the interesting thing is that this, which would have satisfied the ambitions of any young man however determined he was to get on in the world, according to Gurdjieff himself, did not correspond to his own ambitions. He wanted to become altogether Western. This is very understandable, and anyone of us who has been in the Asiatic countries, knows this strange craze that there is for becoming 'technical,' for turning young men into engineers or scientists, when they have talents of quite a different order. Gurdjieff was caught with the same craze, and wished to become an engineer or technician; but with all that, he came under these influences of the traditions, and they would not leave him alone.

We can picture Gurdjieff as a boy under various actions. First, were the severe conditions of his material environment and his human environment; second, the contact that he had with the Western culture through the Russian garrison of Kars, and third, the contact with the older traditions, which were, as he himself said, entirely in conflict with the Westernizing tendencies of the Russians with whom he was in contact. There is no doubt that through being subjected to such contrasting, apparently conflicting influences he was able to come to a realization that there was a great problem; and that is, to account for all the conflicting interpretations of the significance of human life. He was in front of the conflict between the Christian and the Islamic traditions. He was also subjected to the conflict of the kind of dualism which was inherent in the traditions of the Assyrians and the Yezidis, and the unitary traditions which were common to Christians and Muslims and Jews. He saw from early youth, a most significant conflict of beliefs between those of Monotheism and Ditheism; that is, between those who like the Jews, Christians and Muslims believed in one God, Supreme Ruler of the World, and those who like the Zoroastrian dualists believed in two equal and opposite powers. He also stood between East and West at the meeting point of Europe and Asia. He could see for himself how radically different were the two world views and he could also see that with all their divergent views and beliefs men were all the same. He saw spiritual men

14

and materialists, those who looked for reality within and those who trusted only what they could see and hold. Who were right, and where were they all going? Such questions were real and burning questions, and they entered into Gurdjieff's life quite early in his youth.

Was there something in him that was able to see beyond what all those round him were seeing? He had written of his inner conviction that there must be some sense in it all; some sense which would take in the peculiar, even superstitious, beliefs of the old environment, without denying the very striking and extraordinary powers that were undoubtedly possessed by people of that part of the world; giving full weight to the other side, to the increasing domination of the world by the inventiveness and cleverness of man, looked upon at that time as the prerogative of Western Europe.

I think it is not possible to doubt that there was something very unusual in that boy. He himself was a divided character. It is evident from all the accounts he gives of his own boyhood and also from the traces that were left in the later years of his life, that he had in his character very much that we should regard as all too human. He was sensual, loving food, women and beauty, impatient, subject to fits of rage and passion. Moreover, he was ready, in order to satisfy his thirst for knowledge, to be quite unscrupulous in the way he would get it. On the other hand, he never at any time was really interested in possessions or in fame. Undoubtedly, he got himself into trouble more than once in his early years by trying to get knowledge that he was not entitled to, or before he was entitled to it.

With these defects of character, he also had a burning compassion for the sufferings of mankind, all the stronger because he soon became aware that these sufferings are due to our nature. So far as I can make out he was still under thirty when he came to the conclusion that the main cause of human suffering lies in defects that people do not take sufficiently into account. These are, especially, our own credulity and suggestibility, to both of which we are subject because of our vanity and egotism. He realized that we are in slavery to quite trivial and stupid forces that act on us, so that we cannot do the things that we wish to do and we find ourselves doing things that are against everything we hold to be right and to be necessary for man. Gurdjieff saw very deeply the significance of this strange and pitiable condition of mankind. He saw mankind not so much as evil, harmful, or dangerous, but as helpless. This led him to the feeling of a great need to find a way to help people to be delivered of this helplessness.

He also certainly had powers; what are commonly called "psychic powers." These must have been developed in him from unusual potentialities he inherited and was born with. He learned to develop his psychic powers by coming in contact with traditional teachings which, in that part of the world, possess a very extensive practical knowledge of the ways in which man can develop the latent psychic powers. The possession of such powers is a terrible temptation, and Gurdjieff saw that they were both necessary to him and also a danger. One of the touching features of his whole life was what he did to protect himself and others from his own unusual power to influence others. It was touching, because it meant a bitter struggle with his own nature. He must have been very tempted to use these powers for the attainment of his own ends and yet he was ready to sacrifice them quite ruthlessly rather than become their slave. In doing so, he made it impossible for himself to achieve certain tasks he set himself to do. That makes his life very hard to understand, because at times he appeared to be on the verge of achieving something very important and extraordinary, and then something would happen which would change the whole direction of his life. This is common enough with people to whom it happens through some weakness of their own; for example, when they suddenly fail to stand up to the moment of decision and lack in courage or persistence. It was not for such reasons that Gurdjieff failed; it was because of a certain peculiar fastidiousness which was hard to understand for people who only saw him from the outside. He had a certain fastidiousness about using ruthless methods. And that

17

made it very difficult to understand him, because there were times when he really would act so ruthlessly as to terrify those around him. When he acted otherwise, it was not from fear or lack of decision; but from the realization that to take another step would involve him in consequences which might give immediate benefits but would ultimately defeat the higher aim he had set himself.

All of that makes it hard to understand his life and I shall have to talk to you rather specially about the methods that he used in order to protect himself and other people from the powers that he himself had and could exercise. But tonight the main thing is to talk to you about his background, his early environment. So far, I have spoken only about the immediate boyhood environment, that is, the town of Kars, and the surrounding country.

By the time he was fourteen or fifteen, he was already beginning to travel. Not finding the answers to the questions in his own immediate society, not even among these cultivated Russians of the army of occupation in Kars, he began to look further afield. He certainly went both to Nakhichevan and Tabriz. Tabriz is very near to the frontier of Persia and it is very much a Turkish town. The people talk Turkish and are more of the Turkish race than Persian. In Tabriz and the mountains that surround it, there certainly has been a long persistent tradition - probably going back 3 or 4,000 years

– and for people who have the good fortune to come in contact with it, there is still very much to be found in that part of the world. Gurdjieff has left clear indications that he found something important in North-West Persia.

Gurdjieff was also fascinated by his own maternal ancestry; that is, by the Armenians. The Armenians, during one period of the history of man, did carry a special torch, a certain culture, between the 8th and 19th centuries, that very difficult period for nearly the whole of the world. There were the Bagratid Kings of Ani. Certainly the Armenians did not reach this position of power without a long preparatory period which goes back before the rise of Islam and Gurdjieff was interested in the transition from the Christian epoch in that part of the world to the rise of Islam; because much was destroyed at that time, and what was most important went underground, and remained hidden in secret societies. Gurdjieff, suspecting that they still existed, was very intent upon tracing them. You will see references to this in the Chapter, 'Pogossian,' in his Meetings with Remarkable Men. That led him to a journey down through Kurdistan, round Lake Van, to Mosul on the Tigris.

I have visited Mosul once or twice. It is a city where one gets the impression that there is something ancient, something which has been going on for a very long time; I believe it started long be-

19

fore the rise of Islam, even before Christianity. Nearby are Nineveh and Nimrod, the cities of the Assyrian power; but somehow it is not quite that. The impression that I have myself is of something that withdrew to that part of the world after the downfall of Babylon. Gurdjieff was in quest of this knowledge, which perhaps belonged to the Chaldeans.

I must jump now to another of his early influences; that is, the Greek Orthodox tradition. His own father's family came from the Byzantine Greek people. When the Ottoman Turks conquered Constantinople in 1453, they left the whole structure of the old Byzantine Empire; taking over and adapting to their own needs what was needed to keep it all going. They were at pains to ingratiate themselves with the Greek population, requiring the Greeks for the administration of this vast new empire that they were winning. So that there was a peculiar kind of tension; the Turks needing the Greeks and at the same time there was a resentment against the Greek culture. But it undoubtedly influenced them very greatly and also influenced the Sufis of that time. In a strange way, there was an interplay, and the place where a lot of extraordinary things certainly happened was Caesarea as it was then called, Kayseri now. Caesarea was one of the first cities to be converted to Christianity at the time of the missionary journeys and it is the place where the great Christian saints like St. Basil and St. John Chrysostom and St. Gregory lived and constructed the Liturgy of the Christian Church.

Before Christianity came, Cappadocia was a centre of the cult of Anahita, the Mother Goddess; who, strangely enough, made that very same journey from Persia right through Kars, having invaded and arrived in Asia Minor. With her - that is, with her priests, there came a great body of knowledge, and some of that knowledge, perhaps more than people can readily appreciate, has been brought into the construction of the Christian Liturgy. One could say much about the mystery of this Liturgy, which contains so much knowledge, so many hidden things; for this deeply impressed Gurdjieff and he wanted to understand what was being preserved for mankind behind the ritual of the Church. And for that, he made journeys to the Western world. At that time, there were still monasteries in Cappadocia. They remained from about the third century right on and on and on, through the Byzantine Empire, remaining after the Turkish conquest, right through until our day. For sixteen centuries there was a monastic tradition here in Cappadocia. Then it was abruptly stopped at the time when the whole of the population was expelled in 1925.

I am trying to convey to you what I personally believe, and that is, that there has been much more mutual enrichment of traditions than we usually suppose. This part of the world was a kind of crucible in which different traditions were blended, and out of them have come the forms that we now see as so separate - and even opposed to one another - of the Christian, the Islamic, Assyrian, Zoroastrian traditions and so on. All of this, you can well understand, would make a deep impression on a young man in search of the answer to the question: "Does it all make sense, is there a place for all these aspects of human experience, or must some be accepted and others rejected?" And also, the other question which was so sharp for Gurdjieff, "How is it that mankind, to whom so much has been given by the traditional teachings, and the revelations of the past 4 or 5,000 years, how is it that man has been able to make so little use of what he has received, and how is it that he remains under the domination of forces which are quite alien to the real meaning of his own life?"

I think that these Westward searches of Gurdjieff's brought him still further West; first to Istanbul, then to the Holy Land, to Egypt, and even to Abyssinia, where he found again another place where there are strange contacts with lost traditions. Whether he went any further South into Ethiopia, I do not know, but I do know that Ethiopia was very important to him because to the very end of his life he spoke of his great love for Ethiopia. Once he said that he thought of going to spend the rest of his days there. He said that the two places where he felt he had ties were one, Central Asia, that is, Bokhara, and the other Ethiopia. If that is so and if he was not pulling our legs - which of course he often did - it would mean that his visits to Ethiopia formed quite an important part of his total searches. Then of course there were his searches in Central Asia. About those, because they are closely connected with his subsequent teaching, I have to speak about next week. There is little doubt that it was in Central Asia that he came across what was most distinctive and important in what he subsequently called his 'Ideas,' and other people called his 'System.' It is only by making a fairly thorough search into the Central Asian traditions, that we can hope to answer the question, did all that he taught come from these parts of the world, or was there some - that was distinctively his own.

At this point Mr. Bennett showed twenty pictures of Kars, Ani, etc.

QUESTIONS

Q. May I ask if the Mother Goddess, who is said to be Anahita and was worshipped in that area, is the same as Lilith who was both good and evil?

J.G.B. No, I do not think so. It is the same as Cybele who was brought to Rome. Lilith belonged to a more ancient time than this. The important thing, in my opinion, is that there was a continuous tradition in that part of Cappadocia.

Q. Was Gurdjieff remembered in his own country and territory?

J.G.B. No, there are no Christians left in Kars, as far as I know, not one. When I spoke about him, nobody had heard of his name, and when people heard that I had made this long and arduous journey to this derelict country town out of respect for the memory of Gurdjieff, they thought that I was quite crazy. I should say that I did search for the place referred to in his writings where his first tutor Dean Borsh was buried, but everything was so destroyed and smashed up in 1918 and again in 1920, that nothing can really be traced any more.

I think that Gurdjieff is known a little further East than this, that memories of him remain;

round about Tabriz. The people who might know about Gurdjieff would be some of the Dervish sects of that part of the world, but I did not have time to get in touch with them. This cannot be done in a hurry. Further West, when I was in Istanbul, I did meet and talk both with two or three of the Dervish Brotherhood. They retained very long memories of things that have happened. But I was not really in search of this.

Q. How does it come that <u>Meetings</u> <u>with</u> <u>Remarkable</u> <u>Men</u> was published so long after his death?

J.G.B. He died on October 29th 1949, not fourteen years ago yet. He was not very clear about express-ing his wishes about the publication of his second series, that is <u>Meetings</u> <u>with</u> <u>Remarkable</u> <u>Men</u>, but he was very clear that he wanted the first book, <u>Beelzebub</u>, to be published. He said the <u>Meetings</u> <u>with</u> <u>Remarkable</u> <u>Men</u> was to be read aloud, but only to those who had assimilated <u>Beelzebub</u>. I shall say more about it next week; but it is a much more difficult book than most people realize. Those who have not seen what he is after in this book, and who read it just as a kind of autobiographical account, or as amusing escapades, can have no idea at all of the purpose of the book. Or, if they expect to find in the book some part of his practical teaching, they also are mistaken, because it has no claim to con-tain that. But what it contains is really very important, and hardly anyone has understood this. It is probable that the time was not ready, had not come yet for this. The great thing is that it is now available to all.

Q. You have given us tantalizing things about the contents of the Meetings with Remarkable Men. Can you not say more?

J.G.B. Next Monday I will show you just how I followed up one particular clue and you will see in that how unlikely it is that anyone who has not got considerable knowledge both of Gurdjieff's own ways of doing things and also of this part of the world, would have seen what the clue was. If you see that one there, you will see what is involved in being able to decipher the rest of it, because in reality the Meetings with Remarkable Men is written in a kind of cipher, and one has to know how to decipher it. One may think, why should one bother? That all depends whether you wish to get to the bottom of it or not.

Q. Do you understand the languages spoken in that part of the world?

J.G.B. Yes, that is why I go there. I get stuck if I go further East. Languages make all the difference. All the way across Asia, you can talk Turkish; right past the Caspian Sea, across the Amu Daria, right into Chinese Turkestan they can talk some dialect of Turkish. When I was a young man, if you knew Turkish, you could find people who could understand you all the way from the Adriatic right through to the wall of China. When I was living in that part of the world in 1919-20, I had the job of interviewing the Muslim pilgrims who came through from Central Asia and I was very astonished to find that I could talk to people like Sarts and Uzbegs. I was able to talk with them, because these different Turkish dialects are more like one another certainly than, say, English, Dutch and German. It is worth mentioning that Gurdjieff, who certainly could talk Turkish quite easily, for some reason or other pretended that the language spoken here is Persian. If any of you have read the Introduction to <u>Meetings</u> <u>with</u> <u>Remarkable</u> <u>Men</u>, where he speaks about philological questions, and says how strange it is that in English they use one word to express <u>say</u> or something like this, whereas in Persian they use two quite different words, and he talks of the words <u>diyaram</u> and <u>soilyaram</u>. That is simply a very strange way of writing two perfectly good Turkish words as spoken here in Kars, the Turkish of his boyhood. But in the book he calls it Persian. If you understand why Gurdjieff should pretend that what is perfectly good Turkish is Persian you will understand the way he disguises things, I do not believe myself that he knew so many languages. When I first heard of him in 1919, he was

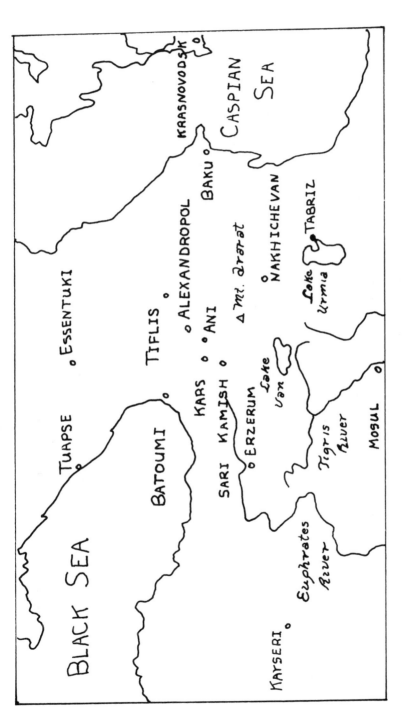

GURDJIEFF'S HOMELAND

THE SOURCE OF GURDJIEFF'S IDEAS

Our next task is the attempt to reconstruct searches that Gurdjieff made between the middle 1880's and about 1910. After 1910, he had found what he was looking for, and was prepared to transmit it to others.

The first thing to remember about Gurdjieff is that he was born of a Greek father and an Armenian mother. Therefore he certainly had contact with the Greek and the Armenian Churches, as well as with the Russian Church - all of which were represented in his home town of Alexandropol and the town where he lived in his early childhood, that is the town of Kars.

There are one or two things I have to say about the influence of such a childhood teaching. To my mind one of the principal differences, psychologically, between the Eastern and the Western Churches, is that the Eastern Church insists principally on the notion of death and resurrection, of dying with Christ and rising again with Christ. This Easter message is the central theme of the Eastern

Church, both in its ritual and also - if one may say so - in its psychology. This has had a visible effect upon people of the Eastern Churches, and accounts for their preoccupation with death and its significance. In the West, we do not have this to the same degree; our Christian belief and our Christian practices are more concerned with sin and redemption, with union with Christ, than with dying and rising again. Substantially, at the bottom, the belief is no doubt the same throughout - I am only speaking now of a particular emphasis, which one feels very much when one is in contact with people of the Eastern Christianity.

There is, I think, also perhaps, in the Eastern Churches a particularly profound sense of the mystery of religion, and of the reality of an unseen element in all religious practice and experience. This does not mean again, of course, that the Western Churches are less mystical than the Eastern Churches, but that the mysticism of the Eastern Churches is more mystery-mysticism than illumination-mysticism, which belongs more to the Western. I think it is fair to say that this early religious background left its mark on Gurdjieff, as it must do on all who are brought up in similar conditions. That is all that I am able to say about this. He himself has said that he continued to be influenced, not only through his boyhood, but later, by his contact with monks of the Orthodox Church - Russian and Greek monks also. He claimed that one of his earliest teachers and friends had entered into a particularly mysterious brotherhood that he called the Brotherhood of the Essenes, of whom he said that their chief monastery still existed not far from the Dead Sea.

It is probable that Gurdjieff retained his contact with the Greek and Russian Orthodox tradition throughout the whole of his life, and certainly when I saw him at the end of his life, the sense that he was a member of the Russian Orthodox Church was quite strong with us. But he was also half Armenian and his mother-religion was the Armenian. This is substantially different from the Greek and Russian, from the Eastern Churches that we commonly regard as 'Orthodox.' The Armenian Church, which has a very ancient Christian tradition, contains elements that perhaps the other Christian Churches have since lost - elements that go back to the early centuries, and belong to that powerful and extraordinary Christian tradition that penetrated from Syria into Mesopotamia, into the old Persia, and right up the valleys of the Euphrates and the Tigris into Central Asia. This very widespread Christian tradition, which was neither Orthodox nor Roman, was overrun by Islam in the 8th century, and has only left traces which we know as the Nestorian and Assyrian Christians. But we must not forget that in the early centuries, this branch of the Christian tradition was as important as either the Greek or the Roman Churches. This was brought home to me when in 1953 I visited

the valleys of the Euphrates and Tigris, and particularly met an extremely learned man – perhaps the
greatest scholar in this particular field – in Mosul.
I was able to enter into that tradition to some extent by visiting some of the oldest monasteries belonging to the Armenian and Assyrian and Nestorian
Christianity – of which of course only the ruins remain at this time – and also by meeting the Nestorians, Assyrian and Armenian Christians.

I am saying all this because I think that we
tend very often to forget that up to the 7th century,
the Christianity of the Middle East was a very important part of the whole Christian life, and only
failed to reintegrate with the West, because of the
arising of Islam and the interpenetration which then
took place between the Islamic, the Persian and the
Christian traditions in that part of the world. We
commonly use the word 'Eastern' for the Greek and
Russian Chruches, and tend to forget the importance
of the Armenian, Assyrian, Nestorian and other
churches of those early days. But certainly Gurdjieff did not forget this, and he was powerfully influenced by the realization that something had been
preserved in the Armenian Church and also among the
Assyrian and Nestorians, which was connected with
the process of spiritual transformation of man, which
they, in their turn, had probably inherited from the
earlier traditions of the Chaldeans, with which, to
a great extent, we have lost contact.

Those of you who have read Gurdjieff's auto-biographical writings, the <u>Meetings</u> <u>with</u> <u>Remarkable</u> <u>Men</u>, recently published in this country, will have noticed how he was convinced that there was a knowledge that belonged to this Assyrian - as he called it Aisor tradition, that was important from the practical point of view. It possessed certain spiritual methods and exercises, and insights into the hidden nature of man, that he could not find in his contact with the now predominant Eastern and Western Christian Churches.

One effect of this was to direct Gurdjieff's attention back towards the past, where he could hope to find perhaps the traces to what was now largely lost. There are others who have come to that conclusion, that the inner, or spiritual, tradition, has largely been lost by the Western Churches - such as, for example, Rene Guenon - but, I am not here to speak about that. I am simply speaking now about Gurdjieff's own situation when he was still a boy between 15 and 18 years old, and experienced the very intense need both to understand the meaning of life and also to find how one could lift oneself out of this situation in which he saw all the people of his environment - Greeks, Armenians, Russians, Tartars, Turks and others.

Now another side of his Armenian parentage, of the contacts that he had through his mother, is the importance among the Armenians of secret societies. Armenians also have an unrivalled talent for keeping out of notice, so that it is only when some unexpected events occur, that cannot be explained by the visible forces, that one begins to suspect that perhaps some pawn has been moved on the board by the hand of an Armenian secret society. I am speaking as one who has lived much in the Near and Middle East - I am not saying that this occurs so much in Western Europe. The point as far as Gurdjieff is concerned, is that through the Armenian secret societies he had an unrivalled opportunity, for a young man, of travelling. This is connected with what I was saying last week, about this extraordinary phenomenon of Gurdjieff's coming out of Kars from the terrible and miserable environment of these invasion-ridden areas of the Caucasus. One contributing factor to his emancipation from this was no doubt the possibility of moving about and opening up contacts quite a considerable distance from his own home, through the Armenian secret societies, sometimes actually as their messenger or representative - as he describes himself in one of the chapters of his book, the chapter called 'Pogossian' his Armenian friend with whom he went first to Etchmiasin, the holy city of the Armenians, and afterwards down to Kurdistan and, according to his own story, ended by going Westward into the Holy Land instead of Eastward into Mosul, as he originally planned. But there is no doubt, of course, that that Eastward journey into Mosul was made later. I have myself heard him speak about Mosul as one of the most interesting and important places in the world still. And I am sure that all of you who have been to that part of the Tigris valley have felt the mystery of Mosul and the surrounding country. It is not just a contact with a dead past, but something which has never ceased and is still somehow there, though perhaps now disappearing. Something still remained in Gurdjieff's time and had been there for not less than 3,000 and perhaps as much as 4,000 years in an unbroken tradition. I know that other people who have been into Mosul and the surrounding country have had the same impression that there is something strange there, if only one could find it. Gurdjieff was not one to have that feeling and not set about in a very determined way to find what he smelt was somewhere hidden. From Mosul Northward into Kurdistan, to Urmia and the crossing into Persia, there has been there probably still is much to be found by people who have the necessary qualities. But I should warn you that these qualities are not given to everyone.

This part of the story is really concerned with the awakening of Gurdjieff to the conviction that a real tradition had existed in the Middle East; possessing knowledge of man, of the world, and also of certain methods and techniques which have remained intact through the great changes due to the invasions that have come from Central Asia and also through the great changes of religion. First, the replacement of the Zoroastrian - the major tradition

- by the Christians, and then again the Christians largely overrun by the Muslim. And yet, through it all, something remained, what is more, as the waves of invasion have come and gone - Genghis Khan and Tamerlane and Atabeg and the rest of them. The waves returning to Central Asia have carried back with them always something, and therefore there is little doubt - and nobody can question that - that in Central Asia, in the parts called Turkestan, there has been and is a tradition which no doubt survived even with the present regime of the Soviet Republic there.

Now, we come to certain more specific indications about the way in which Gurdjieff traced this back and no doubt found something. He travelled with a group of people whom he called 'The Seekers of the Truth,' and some of whom he characterizes quite definitely and has spoken of since as people who were still living even ten or fifteen years ago. Probably the stories told in Meetings with Remarkable Men are genuine enough, though I know, from a certain amount that I have been able to verify, they are all mixed up. In other words, he takes one particular story and puts a bit of it here and another bit there. Certain parts of it also appear in the first book; that is, in Beelzebub, or the first part of All and Everything, which has now been published for thirteen years. There are there - as everyone can see for themselves certain autobiographical sections which are a clue to his own wanderings and his own findings.

One of the things which it is possible to do if you have that luck, or that quality or whatever it is when you are travelling through these parts of the world, is to run unexpectedly into very interesting people. This has happened to me a number of times. I never can understand why it is that something has led me to such a village and I have gone into such a valley and unexpectedly met a person, or I have heard at one place that I ought to go and see so and so and have found a man selling secondhand clothes in a little village, and it turns out that he is an initiated Dervish and so on. These things happen to some people, and they do not happen to other people, I do not know why. I should think they probably happened to me because I had a good deal of preparation and training through my contact with Gurdjieff over so many years. I know that it does happen, and certainly must have happened to Gurdjieff, that in the course of his travels, without any plan, without knowing what he was going to find; he or one of his companions, would hear of something or someone and follow up the clue. This would lead them into the presence of someone who had knowledge, or who had understanding, or perhaps certain powers. Such people very often are not visibly connected with any organization or brotherhood. I have been misled in this way, because I have met people who said that they were not connected with anything at all; just living a solitary and happy life as a recluse in a valley; experiencing the reality of their own inner life or the Presence of God, and not looking for anything more. And then several years later, I would discover that that person, who seemed to be a solitary recluse, was really quite an important member of some brotherhood or other.

Gurdjieff, with his flair for this kind of search, would not only recognize the significance of each such contact; but would also be able to piece the fragments together to build up a coherent picture.

I am now going to tell you about two discoveries which I think will illustrate how Gurdjieff left clues behind so that anyone who diligently and intelligently studies his writings can find some indications; and perhaps - if they feel the need to do so - trace them back to the source. The first is the existence in a region that stretches from East to North-East to North-West Persia across into Kurdistan, of a sect or brotherhood called 'The People of the Truth,' the Ahl-i-Haqq. This sect has been known for a long time. It is referred to in Hastings' Encyclopaedia of Religion and Ethics in several places; but always in passing and rather disparagingly as a heterodox Shiite sect of Persia. It is generally supposed that they are somehow connected with the Ali Ilahis, which is a very extreme Shiite sect who deify Ali, the son-in-law of Muhammad. One would not expect anything of great interest from that, but if you take the fact that they are called 'The People of the

Truth' together with Gurdjieff's reference to his own groups as the 'Seekers of the Truth,' you might perhaps guess that these people, this particular sect, were among those whom Gurdjieff sought and found. It so happens that he does not make any direct reference to a Persian brotherhood in any of his writings that you are likely to have seen, unless you happen to have come across a very rare book published in 1934, called <u>The Herald of Coming Good</u>. This is his first book and the only one published during his lifetime. In it he writes openly of his contact with a brotherhood in Persia, and says that he sent a number of his pupils to their monastery.

Now, I think it is very probable that this brotherhood is the same as the <u>Ahl-i-Haqq</u> with which I accidentally came in contact about seven or eight years ago when I was travelling in North-West Persia and with which I have had further contact since. The important thing about this particular brotherhood is that they certainly are in possession of technical knowledge of a very special kind; that is to say, it is not just a religious, more or less heretical sect of Islam, but it actually does preserve some very ancient traditions. The sect was founded in 1316 A.D. by Sultan Sahaq, but this was more a fresh start or reform than a true beginning. This is evident from the fact that they preserved, through the coming of Islam, not only Nestorian Christian traditions but also much earlier Chaldean or Zoroastrian traditions that had belonged to the time of the greatness of Babylon, which is now 4,000 years before the present. This Gurdjieff does refer to in his book The Herald of Coming Good. I had a very amusing example of the difficulty of knowing where one stands with Gurdjieff over this. One day, in July 1949, when I was with him in Paris, he said that he was going to make some Persian pilaff with real Persian rice which had been flown over to him from Persia. Now we were quite used to Gurdjieff informing us that he was going to bring in some exotic fruit that had been flown to him from the Solomon Islands, when people present in the room had been with him to the Halles that morning and had bought them with him in the French fruit market. When he said that the brinza cheese was specially flown to him from the Caucasus we knew that he always bought it from a particular Jewish shop in Paris. So we were naturally inclined to suppose that it was most unlikely that rice would have been flown to him from Persia. However, I went into his kitchen, and there I saw twenty or thirty little sacks all with labels and Persian stamps on them, and saw that he had, in fact, received by airmail a consignment of Persian rice. What is more, he had received it from the town of Kirmanshah, which happens to be just the very place which is near the centre of this particular brotherhood Ahl-i-Haqq. This may mean anything or nothing, and I must warn you that for anyone who reads Gurdjieff and tries to reconstruct anything about Gurdjieff's adventures, almost anything he writes may mean anything or nothing.

But there are certain much more serious reasons for supposing that there was in North-West Persia at that time – perhaps still is today – a knowledge that contributed towards Gurdjieff's own development. This knowledge is chiefly concerned with the transformation of energies. I am assuming that you would not have come here to hear these lectures unless you were already students of Gurdjieff's ideas and have read his books and the books about him, so I am not going to trouble to explain the teachings and ideas of Gurdjieff, but try to show you how it is possible in some way to follow his method of giving hints so that one can find one's way back to his sources. If so, you must know that a very central feature, or theme, of Gurdjieff's teaching and methods is that man is destined, or required, during his life on earth, to transform energies. One way of looking to see the reason of man's existence on the earth, is that he is able to produce, by his way of living, certain substances required for very high purposes. Man, through his fulfilling this task, receives in return an imperishable something for himself. In other words, that there is the task for man of transforming energies by the way he lives his life. That transformation, in some way or another, results in a division into three parts: one part of the energy has to be used up in performing the work that is needed; a second part of the energy goes to a particular purpose, where it is required; but the third part is his own reward, and enters into his own being and serves for the formation of his own vessel, or his own soul.

Now this goes back into the past - I think that this doctrine was held by the Chaldeans up to the time of the destruction of Babylon, and probably after that remained with the Eastern Christians about which I was talking to you - this required that there should be some knowledge of the sort of work, of the way of living, that makes it possible for man to fulfill this task. It is rather interesting, I think, to note that this is most specifically and clearly understood among the Christians of the old Tradition of the Near East. It is also understood by the Orthodox Christians but less understood by the Western Christians. For example, the Eastern Fathers, and particularly I think, the Russians, understood very clearly that there is something that is required of man of this kind, and they associated it with the idea of, that is, in order to participate in the Resurrection, a man has to acquire a Resurrection Body. Of course St. Paul teaches this in his epistles - but this notion of the need to acquire for oneself a Resurrection Body in order to participate in the Resurrection, was, I think, most strongly and clearly perceived, in the Eastern Christian world. And of course, this agrees with the interpretation given by the Eastern Christians of the Parable of the Wedding Garment; that there are two elements in salvation: there is the gratuitous acceptance of man through his Redemption whereby he is enabled to participate in the Feast, but there is also the requirement that is placed upon man himself, that he should come to the Feast with the Wedding Garment, which is interpreted as meaning the Resurrection Body. And that Resurrection Body is associated with the idea of the transformation of the fine spiritual substances that are exempt from the destructive forces of this earthly existence, and therefore able to participate in Ressurection.

This, I am sure, is somehow connected with the knowledge that is possessed by the Ahl-i-Haqq of whom I have spoken. It seems that they know the ways by which these energy transformations are brought about; that is, by which man is able, by his own way of living - which of course can take the outward forms of prayer and meditation but in reality consist in bringing about within himself a certain interaction of substances - whereby he fulfils his own particular task. All of you who have read Gurdjieff's writings will recognize that this is a central theme. He refers to it as the Reciprocal Maintenance of Everything that Exists. According to this principle everything that exists is required to contribute towards the existence of everything else. There is a close and intimate interlocking of all lives and all forms of life, by which each one is required to do something for every other. What has to be done in this way depends upon the transformation of energy. My own guess is that this is something Gurdjieff learnt through contacts made in those parts of the Middle East that for millennia have been called Iran. Hence also his deep interest in Babylon. Nobody can read what Gurdjieff writes about Babylon without seeing how deeply it impressed him. He was very fortunate because he was able to visit Babylon at the time the German excavations were in progress and when a great deal more of the old city was accessible than it is now. Fortunately for me, those excavations were made in the old style, that is, instead of shutting everything up after digging it out, they left it open, and so I was able to wander about in Babylon and get impressions from it.

I do not know if those of you who know Babylon have had so strongly as I had, the conviction that a certain substance does remain now in Babylon by which one can enter directly into contact with the life of the people about 2,500 to 3,000 years ago. Each time I have been to Babylon, I have had this unmistakably. I have been with others, and I have noticed that some people notice nothing at all when they go to Babylon; they see only a rather dull lot of ruins. Other people are overwhelmed by the sense of the unbroken life that is still going on in this place that has been deserted for a thousand odd years. Why is that? I think it is because there has been for a very long time in this part of the world, understanding of these substances and energies, and that the Babylonians did understand this. This work was intensively carried on in certain areas of Babylon, and it left behind almost imperishable traces of that particular work. This makes it possible for people, even today, to re-enter into contact with what was going on 2,500 or 3,000 years ago. In a sense it is still going on today.

You know that in <u>All</u> and <u>Everything</u> Gurdjieff describes several times the visits of Beelzebub in Babylon. They are among the most vivid writings in the book, and there are hardly any other places in the world that he describes with such a sense of being present in them. I did not see the significance of this until I visited Babylon myself and had the same sense of being able to be present in the living city. I thought how easy it must have been for Gurdjieff to re-enter the life of Babylon and meet the Babylonian people, and know the way they spoke and the sort of lives they lived and what were the motives that governed them and so on. And of course, all this would establish in him very strongly the sense of the importance of understanding how these transformations were to be brought about; how man really could learn to gain control over these psychic and spiritual energies or finer substances, both for his own benefit, for the feeding of his own individuality and also for the accomplishment of tasks that had to be done in the world. And also for other purposes too, such as the helping of individual people.

Gurdjieff undoubtedly had great natural gifts from childhood: but he probably was able as a very young man to develop, through his contact with these sources of knowledge, his powers to a considerable degree and then began to go further afield, having the sure and right instinct that a deeper and more important knowledge existed in Central Asia.

In order to be able to travel, in order to be able to make the necessary contacts, he tells us that he set himself up as a professional healer sometimes even as a professional wonder-worker, or miracle-man, and sometimes just as a hypnotist. He describes how very much he was able to do in Central Asia where at that time there was a very great addiction in the Russian areas to alcoholism, and in the Central and Eastern parts to opium smoking. Opium makes a special impression, I have been through miles and miles of poppy field in that part of the world, and was made to feel how strange and important is the place of the poppy plant for understanding human life. What it has done for man - opening up new possibilities for him, and also the terrible results of misusing the particular fine substance which is produced by the poppy plant. Anyhow, whatever it is, there is no doubt that Gurdjieff at the end of the last century, as a very young man, had found, through his knowledge of these transformations of substances, that he was able to help people with these two curses; the Russian curse of alcoholism and the Asiatic curse of addiction to opium. I myself remember, when I first met him in Istanbul in 1920, how he had in hand a most difficult and extraordinary case, when he cured a drunkard who was considered to be totally incurable.

This phase of Gurdjieff's life between 1895 and 1900 must certainly have been very extraordinary. Sometimes he was just going about in this part of the world with his fluent knowledge of Turkish, no doubt acquiring all the time facility with the various dialects of the Sart, the Uzbek, the Uigur and other races of Turkestan, and becoming known as a man who could help with what we now call psychosomatic ailments of man. In this he was motivated partly by the very real desire to help and do good to people, but more strongly by the necessity for understanding the hidden parts of the human psyche, which ordinarily are hidden behind the mask of our personality, and out of the reach of our ordinary consciousness. It is well known that this mask is either weakened or sometimes even destroyed in conditions of alcoholism and severe drug-addiction when something totally different very often appears. It certainly can be a means for more rapidly understanding the human psyche. Obviously, if Gurdjieff had the power to help people under those conditions, he would also become like a confidant or confessor to them. Many people would come to him in need, and in that way, during those years, he was undoubtedly engaged in what one might call the study of practical psychology. He himself says that before he started on these journeys and before he made his headquarters in Turkestan, he had studied everything that he could of Western psychology and had come to the conclusions that it had very little to offer in the way of explanations. I must remind you that

48

this refers to Western psychology as it was in the 1890's.

He tells us that at some time or other, about the turn of the century, he was in Tibet. I think this is probably true, as I am sure that he knew more than a smattering of Tibetan. Colloquial Tibetan is not difficult to learn. It is mainly a matter of vocabulary because the colloquial grammar of Tibetan is easy. If you do not want to learn to write it - which is a nightmare - to talk Tibetan is simple. I am sure it was well within Gurdjieff's compass to become familiar enough. Of course, Tibetan is not spoken only in Tibet. It is spoken on the other side of the mountains in Turkestan. It is also spoken southward in Nepal, as I have seen for myself. So it is a fairly widely-spoken language in one or other of its dialects, and would come in extremely useful for anyone wishing to travel in that part of the world.

Gurdjieff's visits to Tibet between 1899 and 1902 are connected with one of his severe accidents. He describes in one of the writings of the Third Series how he was wounded by a stray bullet during the Tibetan expedition. This made it necessary for him to spend a long time in recovering his strength. He was again severely wounded in 1904, at the time of the abortive Russian Revolution in the Caucasus - always, as he says, by stray bullets. Each time, apparently, he went to Central Asia where he had friends who understood about the curing of people

49

through the use of these energies and substances. According to his own account, his injuries were such that without this sort of help, he would have died before he was thirty.

Now comes a very interesting question. I have spoken until now of the techniques connected with energies, with the transformation of substances and the deep study of human psychology by the use of Gurdjieff's knowledge of hypnotism and his power to deal with the troubles of mankind. But he also had a very extraordinary and profound knowledge of laws of the structure of the world and the human psyche. One must ask oneself; Where could he have found this knowledge?

When we were interested in these subjects in the middle 1920's, a group of us tried to trace, if possible, the sources of Gurdjieff's notions about Cosmic Laws. For example, his idea of what is called 'The Table of Hydrogens,' that is, the range of substances, from the finest, or Divine Substance, down to the coarsest substance that he called 'Matter without the Holy Ghost.' No doubt you are familiar with this from Ouspensky and Nicoll. Now obviously, this can be directly connected with Plato, and with the sesquialteral calculations given in Plato's _Timaeus_ to arrive at the substances by which the Demiurge made the different worlds. These Platonic notions, after passing through neo-Platonism, entered into various semi-occult traditions such as the Rosicrucians of Europe and Free-Masonry, and more generally with what is commonly called occult tradition. The obvious similarity of these notions and the use made of them by the Rosicrucian authors of the 16th century, such as Dr. Robert Fludd, would make one at first think that Gurdjieff's cosmology is nothing more than an ingenious use of the Rosicrucian material of the 16th century, particularly that of the very important and powerful Rosicrucian School that existed in Holland at that time, of which Dr. Fludd was probably an associate member.

We read as much as we could of this rather laborious material – laborious because it is nearly all written in Latin, but fortunately with ample diagrams. And of course there is the well known _Aurora_ of Jacob Bohme, with the remarkable diagrams constructed by William Law. I expect that this is the material on which Gurdjieff drew. But we came to a stop at a certain point; when we realized that there was no indication of an understanding of what Gurdjieff called the Enneagram, or the nine-lined symbol which he used for the expression of this material. And, most important of all – although you do find in these Rosicrucian writers, particularly, let us say, in Dr. Fludd – the musical scale used, even three octaves in the way Gurdjieff uses them; there is no indication anywhere that the significance of what Gurdjieff calls the intervals, is understood in the way that Gurdjieff understood it. The important point for him is that it is necessary that there should be shocks, or independent interventions, in order to complete any process. This is really of very great importance, and I know from my own studies over many years that there is no doubt that by this a most important light is thrown upon our own personal experience, on the success and failure of all sorts of human enterprises, upon an understanding of the nature of living organisms and of the universe as a whole. All of this is only feebly understood if one does not take intervals and shocks into account.

It happened that just today - quite by accident not intending to read anything of this kind - I read the concluding passages of Kepler's treatise on the movements of the planets. His work, as you know, was largely based upon the feeling that these Rosicrucian constructions must have cosmological significance. I had never previously read the final hymn with which Kepler ends his book.* I had not realized how extraordinary was Kepler's attitude towards his own work. Kepler was looking for something. He, and also, of course, our own Isaac

---

*

The book is Johannes Kepler's Cosmographic Treatise containing the Secret of the Universe based on numbers and the sizes of the celestial spheres - all explained in terms of the five regular geometric figures. Tubingen 1596. This amazing document is translated by I. de Lubicz in "The Egyptian Miracle," pp. 151-163.

Newton, all of these men who founded the mechanical sciences and modern mathematics and astronomy; all of them were inspired by the belief that there was a Law of Harmony. Newton's library contained almost everything that was available at that time on this field - yet there was no sign that he knew this particular secret of the discontinuity of transitions and the need for shocks.

Now that does raise a really interesting question. Where did Gurdjieff find this if it was not known at the time when European thought was most closely concerned with this particular problem, that is, in the 16th and 17th centuries? Why is it that there is no sign among the neo-Platonists and no sign in pseudo-Dionysius, or in the Rosicrucian or Masonic traditions, of an understanding of the necessity of an interlocking play of processes in the way that Gurdjieff represents it in his symbol of the Enneagram?

Gurdjieff himself gives a clue to the solution because both in his book, _Beelzebub_ and also in the writings of the second series, particularly in the chapter called 'Prince Yuri Lubovedsky,' he describes how he found his way to a particular brotherhood which he said was in Upper Bokhara, where this particular knowledge was available. You may not see that he refers to this particular knowledge - but if you will read again the section of the chapter which deals with the training of the priestesses who performed the sacred dances, and the apparatus that they used for their training, you will see that this is an unmistakable reference to this symbol of the Enneagram. Just in case any of you do not know this symbol, I will draw it on the board. It is made by taking a circle and dividing it into nine equal parts. The nine points are joined to give a triangle and a six-sided figure.

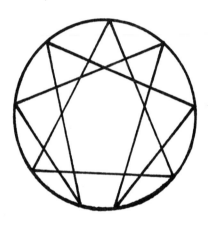

This is Gurdjieff's symbol of the Enneagram, which as you see, combines the triad and the hexad. The secret of the latter lies in the order of the points: 1, 4, 2, 8, 5, 7. The symbol shows how it is necessary that processes should lock together, each one supporting the other in order that anything stable should be achieved. This gives, for example, the stability of a living organism such as the body of man.

I think you will agree that if we could only establish where Gurdjieff found the Enneagram, we would understand where he found what is most important about the content of his teaching. It would tell us where he found that which is missing in the Western Tradition.

Now I have to tell you a very interesting sort of detective-story. Gurdjieff, in the story of 'Soloviev,' which is inserted in the middle of the Lubovedsky chapter, speaks of his being put on the way of finding what he himself was looking for and also of finding his own friend, Prince Yuri, through contact with a Bokharian Dervish, who is called Bogga-Eddin. Now Bogga-Eddin clearly was a Muslim, but there is no Muslim name Bogga-Eddin. There is no problem here, because Russians almost invariably transliterate H by G - they say 'gospital' when we say 'hospital,' for example - and they would almost certainly transliterate Bahauddin as Bogga-Eddin. Therefore, when Gurdjieff speaks of a Bokharian Dervish Bogga-Eddin, undoubtedly he is referring to someone called Bahauddin. Now, there is one extremely famous Bahauddin Naqshbandi of Bokhara, whose tomb there is famous in all Asia, and who is so venerated from the 14th century onward that it is said by Paul Vambery that three visits to the tomb of Mohammed Bahauddin Naqshbandi would be equivalent to a pilgrimage to Mecca.

So I think it is pretty certain that when Gurd-jieff writes about the Bokharian Dervish Bogga-Eddin, he is putting us on to the Naqshbandi Order of Dervishes. Now, I must tell you that the Naqshbandi Order of Dervishes has fascinated me for many years. I have come across them all over the world. Many of you have probably not even heard of the Naqshbandi before you heard me speak about them. Many people have heard of the Mevlevi, or Whirling Dervishes, the Rufai, or Howling Dervishes, or the Kadiri Dervishes, descended from Abdul Kadir Jelani; but I would be surprised - unless you have travelled in those parts - that you have heard much about the Naqshbandi. And yet, the Naqshbandi Order is at this present time by far the most widely distributed of all the Dervish Orders. Naqshbandi Dervishes can be found all the way from Morocco right through to Indonesia. This latter I happened to learn through Mohammed Subuh, who himself went as a boy to study with the most famous Naqshbandi Dervish Sheikh in Java called Abdurrahman. I believe that I am right in saying that there are Naqshbandi Dervishes even in the Solomon Islands. They certainly are in Pakistan, because I have come across them there, and of course all through the Near and Middle East. I believe that they are in Muslim Africa from something I have heard, but I will only speak from my own personal experience. I have met Naqshbandi

Dervishes in Syria, in Damascus and in Aleppo. I have met them in Asia Minor. They may be distinguished from most of the Dervish Orders by certain striking characteristics. First of all, it is a principle of the Naqshbandi Order of Dervishes that man should aim at a complete harmony between his inner and outer life, and therefore they do not allow their own followers to withdraw in any way from the world. Wherever I have met Naqshbandi Dervishes, they have always been people engaged in the ordinary vocations of life - some rich, some poor, some learned, some very simple people, but always living an ordinary life; marrying, having children if it suits them, and prospering in the world, and also there is the very strong principle of mutual love and brotherhood which requires that they not only help other members of the same order but that they should always work for the good of their fellowmen round them. You will certainly recognize that all this corresponds to what Gurdjieff called the "Fourth Way."

The Naqshbandi Dervishes also - I may say this right away because I have seen this for myself - have considerable knowledge of techniques connected with the transformation of energy. There is, however, one very peculiar feature that I found it hard to fathom, and that is that one can never get any Naqshbandi Sheikh to tell you what is behind him; on the contrary, he will either tell you outright, or give you to understand, that he is the centre of their work. His pupils will assure you that he is the one Great Teacher and that there is no other. That is even when one knows that perhaps a mile or two away on the other side of a hill, there is another Naqshbandi Sheikh who is also regarded as the one and only teacher by his followers - as I have seen with my own eyes. One might think, well they are a funny lot, if the Naqshbandi Sheikhs all put themselves up as the one and only. There are only two places where I have come across Naqshbandis where I was told that there was a teacher beyond. That was once in Cehan and once in Istanbul. Always the finger was pointing towards the East. In each case I was told of a particular town. I was even told how, if I was prepared to do it, I could find my way to the Mutessarif-i-Zeman or Teacher of the Time. But I am pretty confident that even if I had found him there would still have remained a certain mystery; and one is inclined to ask oneself whether the Naqshbandi Order is really a prodigious secret society, hiding its organization very successfully by this device of appearing, wherever you touch it, to be at the centre, or whether in the nature of their work, and of their approach to the problem of life, there is this considerable degree of autonomy among the Sheikhs, or leaders or teachers. I think it is the latter. I think that the Naqshbandi Order is not an hierarchical one in the sense that there is a chain of authority. I think that it is quite true that they are more or less independent. Here again we have a characteristic feature of Fourth Way Schools as described by Gurdjieff. They are not 'permanent' or

58

'fixed'; but appear and disappear according to the needs of time and place. Nevertheless, Gurdjieff insisted that there is always an 'Inner Circle' accessible only to those who are able to serve its needs and tasks.

Now Gurdjieff was very emphatic when he spoke to us about all this. He said that the real place to go to is Bokhara. "If you really want to know the secrets of Islam," he said, "you will find them in Bokhara." This is equivalent to saying you will find them if you can find the centre of the Naqshbandi. It seemed clear enough from what he had said about this that these are the people who know about the Enneagram and who therefore have some very profound and extraordinary teachings.

I can point to another piece of evidence that confirms this interpretation, and this is to be found in the etymology of the word, Naqshband. The Order was founded in the fourteenth century by Muhammad Bahauddin who died in A.D. 1390. The Order is not so very ancient compared with the Mevlevis who are contemporaries of the Franciscans or the Kadiris who are nearly as old as the Benedictines. What made Bahauddin assume the surname Naqshband? The word Naqsh means a seal, or a symbol, or sign, and Naqshband means one who seals or makes a sign. The word Naqshband can also be understood to mean those who make symbols, those who have the power to create a symbolism. It seems probable that Gurdjieff, when he was travelling in those parts at the end of the last and the beginning of this century, succeeded in making contact with these people and that he did so. He gives various hints as to what happened. These are distributed round chapters of his books, some in the chapter called, The Bokharian Dervish Hadji Asvatz Troov, some in the chapters that I have already referred to in the second series called, Prince Yuri Lubovedsky, others again in the chapter called, Professor Skridlov, which is the last chapter that has been published. In this way, we reach the conclusion that the knowledge that Gurdjieff afterwards taught as his 'Ideas' came from putting together two halves of a single truth. One half is found in the Western - chiefly Platonic - tradition and the other half is in the Eastern - chiefly Naqshband - tradition. This fusion of two halves is strongly hinted by Gurdjieff in the story of Boolmarshano in Chapter 44 of Beelzebub.

If this is right, then it means that at some fairly early date - before the coming of Christianity - there existed a great knowledge of the construction of the natural order and that this knowledge divided in some way; part of it coming to the West - almost certainly through Pythagoras as Plato suggests in the Timaeus - and partly remaining in the East among the Chaldean Magi and moving up Northward when there was the break-up of the Achimenean Empire after Alexander's invasion. Some things that Gurdjieff spoke about, as when he said, "This that I am telling you now is very old, 4,500 years old," one may judge to be hyperbolical; but I believe it was most likely that he was in fact referring to the start of all this, when the Sumerian culture passed over into the beginning of what subsequently became the Chaldean culture. Probably very much more had been understood at that time about laws and the nature of man than we at present would be ready to believe. You may think that it is scarcely credible that things should be known by these "primitive" people, but if you actually see what they accomplished, you will not regard them as so primitive. If you look also at Egypt alongside and you ask yourself, "What was the relationship between the Sumerians and the Egyptians at the beginning of the third millenium B.C.?" then you may come to the conclusion that a very great deal was known at that time. Maybe we stand on their shoulders with all our modern science to a greater extent than we realize. We imagine that we - in the last three or four hundred years - have discovered practically everything that matters, just from nothing; from the ignorant astrologers and alchemists and the arbitrary and artificial speculations of the neo-Platonists.

Probably behind all this, there was a good deal more real knowledge about man and about the world than we are yet ready to admit.

Gurdjieff was certainly convinced of this, and he did, in his searching, set himself to unearth as much as he could. I have spoken to you this evening, mainly about his searchings in Central Asia, but I know that he also went down to Ethiopia and that he went very much further East. From the way he spoke he must have known the Pacific Islands - certainly the Solomon Islands, from having personally visited them. When he went to the Solomon Islands, he went in search of something, and there is something to be found there even now.

Let me now try to put all this a little bit together. His great good fortune, or fate, was that he was able to reach a source of really important traditional knowledge which may, according to my guess, somehow be connected with the Naqshbandi Dervishes. He also was able to find extremely practical and powerful methods for man to produce and control the fine substances that are connected with our psychic and spiritual experiences. He also did reach - chiefly, I suppose, by his own determined investigations - a very deep knowledge of the human psyche, rather different, and in some ways much more penetrating than that which Western psychology has found over the last sixty years.

Looking back now over some 43 years since I first came in contact with Gurdjieff, I am astonished to see how many of the things that then seemed outrageous contradictions of what was currently accepted by science and psychology have now come to be accepted. This is only in part due to Gurdjieff's own influence – but mainly because of the actual progress of these sciences themselves. It is striking, and I could give you a number of examples of things that seemed to us really strange when we heard them in 1921 or 22. For example, about the nature of extra-galactic space, the countless galaxies outside our galaxy. At that time – I cannot remember exactly when this was beginning to be accepted – but it was already strange to us then. It has now become commonplace.

Next week I am going to speak about the problem of deciding whether all that Gurdjieff produced was simply the result of his own researches, very cleverly put together by the concerted efforts of a group of quite outstanding men, or whether there is something more that cannot wholly be reduced to terms of a prodigious research into tradition and of an almost equally prodigious effort of synthesis. I have told you the story as far as I can tonight. Next week I am going to speak more about his actual teaching and methods from the time that he gegan to teach to the end of his life. I shall also say what I believe he really intended should come out of his work.

If I have spoken about things with which, because you have not read about them, you are not familiar, I hope you will forgive me; I thought that the advertisements about these lectures would not be likely to attract people who had not already a

QUESTIONS

Q. I am Armenian myself, but I am not familiar with the Armenian secret societies you referred to....

J.G.B. At least you are familiar with the Dashnak?

Q. That was a political part.

J.G.B. Much more than that.

Q. But not on the Mystical side?

J.G.B. All that I can say is that I personally have been in contact with people in 1919 and I am sure that there was also a mystical element in it. It appears on one side as a political party as I said. I had that real evidence about this from the Caucasus, there was also a religious and even mystical element.

Q. But the Dashnak is a political party founded with Marxism, and this is hardly mystical.

J.G.B. It only became a political party long after the time I am speaking of. In 1920 it was still a secret society. I can only tell you about people that I personally met when I was in Istanbul in 1919 and 1920. These people who were members of the Dashnak then were certainly not Marxists, that I can tell you for reasons that are quite categorical. The outward aim of the Dashnak was to secure the independence of Armenia. It was an Armenian nationalist movement, not political in the sense of being either Marxist or anti-Marxist at least at that time. I am perfectly confident that if you go back to the 1890's, when such societies already existed, that then they were simply to defend the Armenian way of life.

Of course, it is perfectly true that they were a thorn in the flesh of the Tzarist Russian government of that time. But why? Because they wanted the independence of Armenia; they were also a thorn in the flesh for the Turkish government for the same reason. But this was only one side of it. What I do know from what Gurdjieff himself said about it, this part at least is verifiable - that the possibility that he had of travelling through what is now Armenia, and through Kurdistan, arose through his connection with one or other of these societies.

Q. Is anything known about his stay in India?

J.G.B. Very little. Only one, no doubt, totally apocryphal story of his own, that he met Madame Blavatsky when he was a boy of 17 or 18, and that Madame Blavatsky fell in love with him.

Q. Has the Enneagram definite characteristics? Is it a symbol of a society similar to the Pentagram?

66

Has it any connection with others?

J.G.B. Very probably it is the emblem of a society. I am not now concerned with the interpretation, but I will certainly have something to say about it next week. I am only talking at the moment about its being a symbol, or Naqsh, that may be connected with a society, rather than with its being an instrument. The only time that I have heard of this apart from Gurdjieff's own reference as to its connection with the Bokharian Dervishes, is that somewhere in North India it is still used as an instrument for divination.

Q. Could you say something about the techniques for transforming energy?

J.G.B. All the part concerned with how he taught and what he taught I am reserving for the third lecture. Tonight I have been trying to indicate what appeared to be the probable sources and how he came to the material that he subsequently called his 'Ideas' or his 'System.' Of course, I shall have to speak about the transformation of energy next time to complete this very cursory presentation of the enigma of Gurdjieff. But you understand that I am not giving lectures on Gurdjieff's teaching so much as trying to show something about the strangeness of this man. Many, many people have travelled in these parts of the world, and nobody seems to have found the things that he found. At one time,

I and many others, thought that it was something that he got from Western Traditions, and no doubt there have been Russian occultist societies that made an immensely diligent search of the material which fascinated many Russians at the end of the 19th century and the beginning of this century. It was only when we began to make a serious study of this in 1924, that we came to the conclusion that this was certainly not the explanation, that Gurdjieff must have found something quite different from what was available in Europe, and also quite apart from anything that was available in India - for it is not like the Tantric, or Buddhic, or what are known as the Theosophical sources. I have not spoken about all that tonight because that is mainly negative; but there are certain points of contact. Undoubtedly Gurdjieff has studied Buddhism quite seriously because there are certain features of Buddhist psychology that he has adopted and weaved into his own ideas. But these sort of more fundamental notions are not to be found, so far as I am aware, either in any of the classical Hindu philosophies or in the Tantra, or in Buddhism.

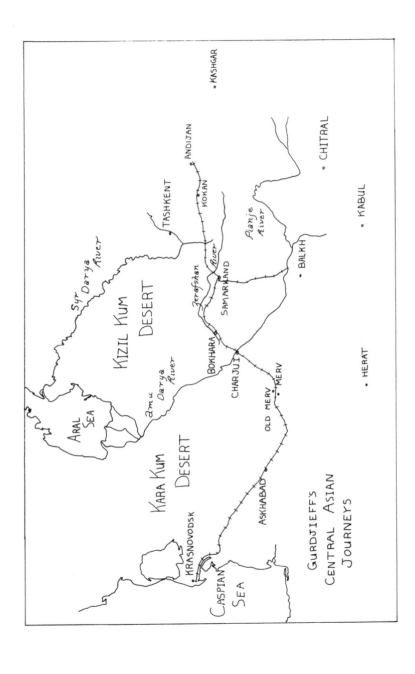

GURDJIEFF'S
CENTRAL ASIAN
JOURNEYS

GURDJIEFF'S TEACHING AND METHODS

A striking characteristic of Gurdjieff's teaching and methods is that he never stood still. To the very end of his life he was experimenting and there was no stationary period, so far as I have been able to make out, from the time he began his active searches at the age of about 16, that is, about 1888, right up to the end of his life, in October 1949.

Experimentation can lead to misunderstanding because people acquainted with one particular period of his life may take it as being representative of the whole; and find themselves in complete contradiction with people who know a different period of his life. This also concerns statements which he made at one time, which might be thrown aside and contradicted thirty years or even thirty days later. Most of the books that have been written about Gurdjieff refer to particular periods of his life and therefore one cannot get an adequate picture from reading books alone.

There is one other characteristic of Gurdjieff that I must refer to at once; and that is, his adoption of a deliberate disguise in the form of putting himself in a bad light. He put on a mask that would tend to put people off, rather than draw them towards him. Now, this method - which is called by the Sufis, the Way of Malamat, or the methods of Blame - was highly esteemed in old times among the Sufis, who regarded the Sheikhs or Pirs who went by the Way of Blame, as particularly eminent in spirituality. Such people represented themselves to the outside world under a bad light, partly in order to avoid attracting praise and admiration towards themselves, and also partly as a personal protection. This way of Malamat has been lost to sight in modern times. It was certainly followed under other names in Christianity also and in all the great ways of religion. The attraction to oneself of blame rather than praise, has always been approved: but it is not very much understood at our present time, nor is it usually thought right to do so by deliberately performing blameworthy actions.

There is a particular reason for following the Way of Malamat, connected with the powers that surround people destined for a high eminence in the world or in spirituality. In the old Zoroastrian teaching, there was recognition of a certain power called Hvareno. This was a mark of kingship, and whoever had Hvareno had the power of attraction over people. He had the 'royal touch.' The same power was recognizable by certain marks or features of the physical body. These marks showed a man destined for a very high advancement which could either be material or spiritual. For example, the Buddha was said to bear such marks; which were recognized, when he was still a child. They showed that he was destined for a very high degree of spiritual advancement. It was not possible to tell whether this meant that he would become a great king destined to rule the world or that he would become a great spiritual Initiate. If a man bearing those marks, or having the power called Hvareno, wished to follow the way of spirituality, then he had to protect himself against being drawn into Messiahship, or the outward exaltation of his person. One reason for following the Way of Malamat, among people of very high spiritual destiny, is to protect themselves against being put upon a throne, as it were, and either served, or even worshipped.

The Gospels make it clear that Jesus had this Hvareno to a superlative degree so much so that the Jews wanted to take him by force and make him King. But we are told that each time this was threatened he withdrew and hid himself. This may be taken to mean that Jesus also followed the Way of Malamat expressed in the words, "He was despised and rejected of men." You may remember that in the Imitation of Christ, St. Thomas a Kempis advises Christians who wish to follow Christ to seek blame rather than praise in all that they do.

We may conclude then that the Way of Blame

can belong to the very highest summit of spirituality since even Jesus Christ adopted it in order to fulfil His Mission upon earth. It seems even that it is right for everyone who is in danger of attracting to himself the wrong kind of hero-worship that verges on idolatry. The power of personal attraction is a terrible temptation that few can resist.

Gurdjieff realized at an early age that he did possess powers of this kind. I am not suggesting that Gurdjieff should be compared with Solomon or the Buddha, who are known to have these marks, but simply that he had a certain inborn quality of Hvareno and that he became aware that this quality could result in his coming to a position of external authority. He explains, in the writing to which I referred last week, The Herald of Coming Good, which he wrote in 1933, that twenty-one years earlier that is, in 1912; he decided to adopt what he calls 'an unnatural way of living,' precisely in order to protect himself against the consequences of his own Hvareno.

A man who adopts that particular procedure is very hard to understand in terms of his external behaviour, and this has obviously been the case with Gurdjieff. People have tended to form judgments about him in terms of his outward behaviour, and have failed to take into account the possibility that this outward behaviour was deliberately adopted for the very purpose of which I am speaking now.

He himself referred to this in The Herald of Coming Good; but soon after the publication of this book he suppressed it and withdrew as far as possible all copies from circulation, and probably comparatively few of you have come across it. This also was connected with the same need to disguise his real nature. He decided upon a course of action other than what was foreshadowed at the time that he published this book. This book was a ballon d'essai sent up to ascertain the consequences of announcing to the world that certain things were possible. And when he found that the consequences were such that there would be a serious misunderstanding of what he was attempting to do, he drew back and began to follow a more hidden way.

I think I can assure you from all my studies of his life and my various contacts with him that he really was a man who deliberately chose to hide his own powers behind behaviour that would attract blame. If you reflect on this you will see how very difficult it must be for us to disentangle from the outward show who was the real man and what were his real purposes. Before speaking about these, I must run briefly through the phases of his life during the period of his search; that is, from the age of about fifteen until his death. There were, first, the comparatively local searches and contacts made in that extraordinary region of the Caucasus, the meeting-point of Europe and Asia, where he was born and brought up. Then later, from about the middle 90's until early in the 20th century, he travelled very much more widely. And during this time also, there is no doubt, he spent considerable time in contact with a certain Brotherhood to which he refers a number of times, and where he learnt about an ancient and hidden tradition. This gave a new direction to his subsequent activities. After this period of searching, he entered upon a period of experimentation with the problem he had set himself; of finding a way to deliver mankind from the particular defect in human nature which, as he saw it, was going to be of increasing significance with the way the world was going. That feature of human nature is suggestibility; that is, the weakness of people in front of external suggestion, the tendency to follow the crowd and to be carried away by any kind of propaganda. With the advancing techniques of communication, this has become at the present time a very serious menace to the world. One result of suggestibility, when methods of communication develop, is that personal initiative tends to be stifled, and it becomes possible to control men's minds by suggestion to an extent that can become quite disastrous both to those who submit to control and also to those who exercise it. Aldous Huxley has drawn a picture in <u>Brave</u> <u>New</u> <u>World</u> of the limits to which this could go.

In order to study the problem of human suggestibility, Gurdjieff made profound investigations into hypnotism. In fact, the very first conversation I had with him, in 1920 on the first day I met him was about hypnotism. He then told me such astonishing things that I realized he had far deeper knowledge than anyone I had met. It so happened that in 1920, I was very much interested in this subject. Not only had I read a good deal about hypnotism, but I had also been instructed in it by an expert in the subject and had practised myself in order to see how far it could help me to understand certain conclusions connected with time and eternity which I had reached from mathematical studies, I spoke, therefore, with a certain experience; but it quickly became clear to me that I was a mere infant in the field of hypnotism compared with Gurdjieff. And not only I, but other people who had studied this rather deeply, whom I had personally met, such as Charles Lancelin, the well-known French occultist, were far from understanding what hypnotism could do for man.

Gurdjieff was engaged in the practical study of hypnotism between 1900 and 1908 and, as I said to you last week, he probably worked at this mainly in connection with the curing of people from alcoholism and addiction to opium, and also with various other influences that increase suggestibility and diminish the power of initiative in people.* During those years, Gurdjieff was trying to see whether

* The main source of information about this is The Herald of Coming Good.

76

he could establish a practical means for helping people with this grave human problem. I do not want to imply that suggestibility is the very centre of all man's troubles, because it is a derivative weakness that results from man's own egoism. If it were not for his egoism, he would not be suggestible. Nevertheless, suggestibility is a symptom and a manifestation of weakness that is more serious than most people nowadays are prepared to admit. We hear, of course, of things like brain-washing and propaganda for advertising and political purposes; but, in reality, this vice or weakness of suggestibility is deeper than these and the effect upon the human race will be disastrous unless it is counteracted.

Therefore, when Gurdjieff took as the theme of his study to discover means whereby mankind could be delivered from this psychic weakness, he was concerned with something that is really important for us all. Now, you cannot cure a symptom unless you can do something about the root cause from which this symptom comes. Behind suggestibility, there is a woeful ignorance of human nature, which is one of the awkwardnesses of our present situation. It is awkward just now because we know so very much about external nature, and so very little about internal nature, and this produces a rather threatening imbalance of our activity. We can work so effectively on the outside and remain ineffectual on the inside.

Gurdjieff was thus led to take a deep concern in man's own nature in order to find why people do not know themselves. It is probable that it was in this contact that he made with this particular school of which I was speaking last week, he hit upon the real explanation of this; which is very seldom grasped nowadays, even, for example, by people who have studied Gurdjieff's ideas either in writing or even in practical ways. The basic illusion concerns the nature of consciousness. What we ordinarily call consciousness is only a reflection of consciousness. The true consciousness is the reverse of what men call consciousness. Behind our ordinary consciousness, there is another consciousness, but it is more true to say that what we call consciousness, our ordinary consciousness, is, as it were, a reversal of consciousness, rather like the negative of a photograph where light seems dark and dark seems light.

I think that when Gurdjieff came to understand this characteristic of our consciousness, he then was able to see how his earlier studies of hypnotism really could be fitted into a more complete picture of the human problem. In other words, it was necessary to discover ways by which man could enter into his true consciousness without, of course, losing his contact with the external world, for which we use our reversed consciousness, or, as it is often called, rather misleadingly, lower consciousness.

78

Side by side with these discoveries about human nature, there is no doubt that Gurdjieff was also deeply interested in what he calls the Laws of World Creation and World Maintenance, a name he used to describe the knowledge for which man has always searched that will enable him to understand the world and his place in it. It is the need to learn how the world is constructed and how it works, and why it is that we men are able to be related to our world in the way we are. This is a question that can hardly even be formulated by natural science which studies only that which can be known and not the source of knowledge itself, that is, man's own nature. Science accepts as a given fact that there is a being such as man in the midst of a world governed by laws of physical and chemical and biological processes, about which science cannot answer nor even ask. For that, it is necessary to have a total picture of the world in which man and his experience and the world and its nature are all brought together. It is the need to understand this total situation of man in relation to his total world that drove Gurdjieff towards anything that he could hear about in the nature of fundamental laws or principles and he came across some extraordinary knowledge in this field and was able between 1908 and 1912 to piece together a cosmology that he was never able to complete.

That brings us now to the fifth period of his life, that began about 1910, when Gurdjieff set himself - probably in collaboration with people who had joined him in his searches - to put all this material together; that is, to combine what he had learnt in psychology, in a practical way, particularly in his studies of hypnotism, with what he had learnt about laws and the structure of the world - that is cosmology. And so began to take shape what was later called 'Gurdjieff's System,' but which he himself usually called his <u>Ideas</u>. How long that period of synthetic activity lasted is difficult to say; because in a sense it was still in progress at the beginning of the First World War. By that time he had realized that, in order to make this synthesis, it was necessary to have people upon whom he could experiment. He set himself to found, first of all small groups of people here and there, and later what he called his Institute for the Harmonious Development of Man. He was no doubt connected with very exalted circles right up to the Tzar and his Court. He met Tzar Nicholas II a number of times. He spoke to us of his admiration and compassion for the Tzar and of the strange situation that existed round the Russian Court. As I think you know, his wife was a noble Polish lady from the Imperial Court.

That period, when Gurdjieff moved in rather high circles in Russia, leads up to the beginning of the 1914 war. It is very likely that, as he told us, he was in direct contact with Rasputin, the monk who had such a strange influence over the Russian Court and which Gurdjieff tried to counteract. Afterwards he rather withdrew from all that. Then came another period from 1915 on when Gurdjieff had met Ouspensky and the people that Ouspensky brought to him. During this time he had several experimental groups with which he worked through the war-years from 1915 until the revolution, when he withdrew to the Caucasus. His father was killed in the over-running of Kars by the Turks on 25th April 1918. It happens that we seem to know a good deal about Gurdjieff's activities during the period from 1915-1919 because of what Ouspensky has written in his book, In Search of the Miraculous. We must not forget that Ouspensky was in contact only with a small part of Gurdjieff's work. A number of the experiments that Gurdjieff started were cast aside and he began to work in different ways, so that what he did later represents an entirely new phase.

Now, you may ask, what was he experimenting with? Here I must say something about the very difficult problem of transferring Understanding from one environment to another. There is no doubt that in Asia there is a traditional wisdom of very great importance to mankind. Contrary to what is usually supposed, this is probably more highly developed in what is called the Middle East than in India and the Far East. But it does not really matter where it comes from, the point is that the transferring of this wisdom to our European environment is an exceedingly difficult matter; far more difficult than people suppose. There have been various premature attempts at bringing to the West notions and methods that have come from India, from China, from Japan, from the Middle East - from Buddhist, Hindu, Tantric, Zen, Sufi and other sources. Really serious difficulties have arisen, because those who have made the attempt to bring this wisdom to the West have either been Europeans who had imperfectly assimilated what the East had to give, of Asiatics who did not understand the European and American environment. In nearly every case they made serious mistakes, either in attempting to transfer exactly what worked extremely well under certain Asiatic conditions into quite different conditions, or in adapting it to the West without really having understood the new environment.

One of the chief tasks that Gurdjieff set himself to accomplish was to see how what he had found - particularly in Asia and to a minor extent in Africa - could be made available in a practical way to Western people. It took him something like thirty years of constant experimenting before he arrived at a method that he found reasonably satisfactory; and this in spite of the fact that he started with two considerable advantages. One was that he was, after all, himself of European origin, and the other, that his particular study had been of the defects in human nature that required to be overcome. His studies had not been directed solely to the perfecting of man - for example, by such methods as the direct penetration into the deeper consciousness by meditation - but he had studied deeply the obstacles in our nature that prevent us from living normal lives. This certainly gave him a considerable advantage when he came in contact with Western people because these obstacles are not so very different in East and West. The real difference between the East and West are more in the kind of things that we believe in and the kind of things that they believe in; the kind of things we hope for and the kind of things they hope for. That is why it is difficult for us to understand one another. It is not so much that our natures are different, but rather that we put our trust in things which they would not dream of trusting, and on the other hand they put their trust in things that we would not dream of trusting.

The task Gurdjieff set himself from about 1910, until about the early 1930's, corresponds to that period which I spoke of, when he said that for twenty-one years he set himself to live an unnatural life. Then, for a short time, he began to live normally again, and then afterwards he returned to a way of living difficult to understand.

I must say something now about the final outcome of all this, because I will not have time to speak at any greater length about the stages of his experimenting. You must remember what I said last week about substances, how in the Eastern countries - especially in the Middle East - more is understood about the substances that are behind activities, than we yet understand in the West. Gurdjieff was very clear about the importance for man of being able to produce and control the substances he requires in order to produce changes. He understood that you cannot improve the way something works if you continue to feed it with unsuitable fuel. You have to produce a more refined fuel to get a more refined action.

In connection with substances, there is little doubt that Gurdjieff, somewhere at the beginning of this century, came across a notion which he afterwards wrote about in the chapter called 'War,' of Beelzebub, where he refers to the learned Kurd Aternach, who discovered that the reason for war on earth lies not in the behaviour of human beings, but in the necessity for a particular substance which can only be produced in one of two ways; either by the conscious and intentional activity of people, or by their death. It follows that if people will not produce this substance intentionally, then deaths – and especially premature deaths – have to be increased on the earth. War becomes inevitable on this account. This notion implies that wars are the consequences of man's failure to perform his cosmic duties, and on account of this failure, conditions arise that make war inevitable. Or if not war, the premature dying of people has to be brought about. Since, according to this theory, the required substance is liberated by some kind of death; the result can presumably be obtained by an enormous increase in the world's population such as has occurred during the present century. This is hinted at by Gurdjieff at the end of Chapter XLII of Beelzebub, when he refers to wolves, rats and mice. You are also no doubt aware of the suggestion that this process is somehow connected with 'feeding the moon.'

Whether we take these suggestions literally or figuratively, there is no doubt that Gurdjieff felt that he had come across a truth deeply significant for us all; namely, that man must either perform a certain duty for which he exists on the earth, or else be compelled to live and die in such a way that the results will be obtained from him willy-nilly, in spite of himself.

This notion can be put very simply in this way, that intentional actions, performed for a rightful end, result in a certain substance being released. One part of that substance goes into the performance of the action; one part of the energy becomes available for this purpose, whatever it is; and the third part of the energy becomes available for the perfection, the inner development and spiritualization of the person himself. Human life should be so organized that this transformation of energy is really consciously undertaken by a sufficient number of people, and only in that way can the hazards of human life be averted.*

---

* For more details, read Beelzebub, pp. 1105-8.

This belief, in a slightly different garb, is not unfamiliar in the West in the doctrine of vicarious suffering and the transfer of merits. Gurdjieff regarded it as vital that men should recognize this duty and set themselves to work in such a way that it will be performed. In that way alone can a great danger to mankind be averted. Gurdjieff was concerned to set up conditions in which people could be shown, if they were willing to do it, how this transformation of substances can be undertaken; in other words, how man can perform his cosmic duty. The principle is that, in performing that duty, he both serves his fellow-men and also saves his own soul.

It so happens that this is intimately connected with the problem of suggestibility. A great deal turns upon people understanding that, if they are to perform their cosmic duty, they must liberate themselves from suggestibility. They must be independent and free people; who can freely and consciously assume and accept the duties they have to perform. So it comes to this, that it is necessary to show people how they can free themselves from the illusions and weaknesses that make them suggestible and self-indulgent, and also they must be shown how they can perform the task which is required of man. Of course, this latter can be shown in the form of moral codes, or the teaching and the practice of religion. These collectively constitute what is called the Ways of Objective Morality. Anyone who sincerely and wholeheartedly follows the practice of his or her religion and keeps to its commandments; will produce the very same results as come from the conscious transformation of substances. Their way of living will give what can otherwise be obtained only by dying. Nevertheless, there is both a possibility and a need for a limited number of people to follow what are called the Ways of Accelerated Completion. These ways take different forms: some are connected with religion and others are not, but they all have in common the need for a more exactly and more personally regulated work of transformation than is possible by following rules or commandments formulated for the guidance of all and therefore of necessity very general and often vague. Among the Ways of Accelerated Completion is one called the Fourth Way which is characterized by the fulfilment of all ordinary life obligations, coupled with a very exactly regulated and very intensive personal work.

It will be obvious to anyone who has read Gurdjieff's writings and has some knowledge of his life; that his interest was wholly concentrated upon the Fourth Way. This requires the highest degree of intelligence, adaptability and inner freedom in those who direct it; for they have to create conditions that enable the Duty of Transformation to be performed without neglect of the obligations common to all men and women. This brings us to the simple, practical question: what are the conditions that make it pos-

sible for man to fulfil his cosmic duty? For those
who do not know of the Fourth Way; it must appear
that it is best done in retirement from life. The in-
tensification and acceleration of this work was for-
merly supposed to be the task of monks and recluses,
withdrawn from the world, who could devote the
whole of their time and energy to this action which
brings about the transformation of substances. It is
probably true that this was more generally the case
in earlier times, when the conditions of life on the
earth were much simpler than they are now. But our
present-day problem is different, and Gurdjieff was
well aware that there is a far more intimate interlocking of lives on the earth, due to the progress of
communications and various other technological advances; so that it is no longer possible to rely mainly
upon withdrawal from the world in order to produce
the required results. Therefore, it is necessary that
means should be found whereby people can increase
this work in the ordinary conditions of life. And
this is the so very remarkable thing about the present century, that a number of new movements have
appeared in all different parts of the world, under
different names, connected with all the great re-
ligions of the world, but in every case, there has
been a movement towards the carrying out of one's
spiritual obligations in the ordinary conditions of
life.

You will perhaps conclude that all these
movements belong to what I have called the Fourth

<u>Way</u>. Unfortunately, there are many imitations of this way that entirely lack the quality of <u>accelerated completion</u> which is the only justification for departing from the Ways of Objective Morality. This is a very interesting thing, which I have myself studied, as well as I can. In perhaps twenty or thirty different movements I know of the one really common feature is that they do take as a principle that man can live a complete life, outwardly and inwardly, without withdrawing from the world, and without abandoning the ordinary responsibilities of man - to marry, to bear children, to accomplish certain external work in the world and so on. And yet it can by no means be said that they are all - or even the majority of them part of the Fourth Way. There is far too much theory and too little practice in many of these movements and in others there is a lack of flexibility in method that is quite incompatible with the demands of accelerated completion.

I am not concerned at the moment with the abortive attempts at establishing centres of Fourth Way work, but rather at the widespread recognition that such work is needed. I think that this is not merely a consequence of the changing outlook of the twentieth century, perhaps even the reverse, it may be that our outlook is changing just because this kind of new appreciation is entering. It is felt that people living ordinary lives must be able to make a contribution towards the solution of the great problems of mankind. And so it is that we see for example in the Christian Churches - how the division of priest and layman is diminishing everywhere. There is recognition of the importance of the religious and spiritual life of people who are not, as it were, specialists, i.e. priests; this is now admitted to a degree that would have been unthinkable a hundred years ago. The same is also true in Buddhism. It is much less than a hundred years ago that the only people who were regarded as seriously religious were the monks or Bhikkus. The lay Buddhist was content to live an ordinary life with no expectation of attaining anything, except possibly at some time, reincarnating under conditions that would enable him to withdraw from the world. The cannonical Buddhist books - the Pali Pitakas - are entirely orientated towards that notion of the complete, unquestionable superiority of life of the Bhiddu, of the one who renounces the world, over the life of the ordinary worldly man. To an extraordinary degree, in this XXth century, Buddhism has abandoned this traditional attitude, and there are movements - such as the Satipatthena movement in Burma - which show the ordinary layman how to meditate in such a way that he can be given the expectation of attaining the spiritual development that was previously thought to be reserved to the Bhikku.

Having introduced the notion of the Fourth Way I must refer to another important feature, that, namely, it has no permanent form, no permanent place, no centre. It is constantly searching and adapting itself. It does so, not for the purpose of improving its own content, but for the purpose of performing a task. There is a certain <u>Work</u> to be done in the world, and in order to do that work some people must come to the requisite understanding. People who suffer from suggestibility, from weakness in relation to the external world, who do not know themselves - and especially those who remain in the ordinary reversed consciousness, or semi-consciousness - such people cannot effectively or directly perform this task, with its different specific undertakings. Therefore, it is necessary, for those who have responsibilities in this direction, to help people to prepare themselves if they choose and if they wish to do so.

This leads to a very important distinction. There is primarily this notion which belongs to the twentieth century, that spiritual development does not require, in our time, withdrawal from the responsibilities of life; that is, to make it one's professional job to be spiritual. That is the first thing which is common, as I say, and is permeating everything, both the known religious practices of man and also all kinds of new movements that have arisen. Secondly, and this is less clearly understood, is the notion that accelerated development is associated with the carrying out of certain <u>Work</u>. The notion of the Fourth Way is wholly bound up with these two principles; the first is that of complete involvement in life externally, and secondly, in the acceptance internally of responsibility for certain work that is required for a great Cosmic Purpose

According to Gurdjieff, this purpose is concerned with the transformation of substances whereby the destiny of mankind as a whole can be kept moving in the right way. This takes many forms. It can take the form of activities of artistic creation; it can take the form of certain kinds of social organizations; it can take the forms of the transmission of specialized forms of knowledge, or research into the conditions of mankind, and preparation for the future, and certain other tasks, more specifically connected with what I said; that is, the transformation of substances.

I am personally confident, from long years of study of this matter and having been in contact with a rather unusually large number of people who have been concerned in this particular field, that there really is such Work and that there are people who understand it in a way that is not obviously visible on the surface. This means that there is in effect a Twofold Life on the earth. One is the visible, external life in which we all have to participate, and the other is an invisible life in which we can participate if we choose. In a sense one can say the first life is a causal life; that is to say, in that life causes that exist in the past produce results that are being experienced in the present and which will be carried forward in the future. It can also be called the stream of happenings. It is of course called by such names of Samsara and the Wheel of Life, and so on, but in a very simple way it is the ordinary life that we all live. The second, the other life, is non-causal, which means that it exists only in so far as it is created. It is the life of Creativity. Every creative act rightly performed is a means of participation in that life. And the search for creation is the search for that life.

Creation is infinitely varied in its content and its forms. Everything that is going on everywhere is also a field of possible creativity, and therefore there is no limit to what can be found in the field of creation. But the great majority of mankind are content to live in the first life. A few are searching for the other, because there is a feeling of a need to participate in creative activity and a realization that one is only half alive, and perhaps not even that, if one is not participating.

This is what is meant by the word Work, and when we talk about 'the work' or the Great Work - Magnum Opus - it refers to the invisible world which has to be perpetually created in order that it should be. And it is that that we are called to if we are destined for accelerated completion. In order to enter that world, we have to earn the right to be in it, and for that we have to bring to it something made by ourselves. The first and simplest thing we can bring is our own capacity for work; our own capacity for transforming energy, and therefore for participating in the Creation. This can afterwards be converted into specific forms of creativity, according to objective needs and our own subjective powers.

There is no doubt that the Fourth Way is the direct application of the principle of creativity in life. That is why I called it <u>non-causal</u>. It always has to start without an antecedent cause. It is a spontaneous call from beyond that makes this possible. I am not going into this in detail. I would have to give a philosophical lecture, and I would be in danger of having to answer philosophical questions; but let me just say this simply, that there is a Work to be done, and that some people have the feeling that their life is not complete unless they are participating in that Work. It is to such people that these lectures are addressed.

Gurdjieff found a direct way of participating and he tried to bring this in such a form that it should be available to us, to people of our Western world. He certainly did not create this form, nor was he the founder of this way - but, I think there are probably certain things connected with this where Gurdjieff had a sort of special inspiration connected with the transition from the past to the new epoch into which mankind is now entering. What is significant about the future of our world is the coming unification of every form of human experience. The Work is concerned with bringing people together and not with separating them. I am sure that this is a very visible characteristic of this twentieth century of ours. In one way, this obligation to unite stirs up most serious reactions, and therefore we have seen troublesome wars and hostilities and hatreds. But if you look behind all this, you can see they all come about because there is an urge to unite and not to isolate. One very obvious feature of this is the increase in tolerance that has come over the world, and the mutual acceptance by people which is perhaps the most hopeful and admirable feature of our century, with all its depressing features.

Now, what does this add up to in practice for us, and what was Gurdjieff really after? There is a very interesting hint that he gives – I think it is not in any of the published writings about it - in certain lectures that he gave in New York in the early 1930's, and he refers to it very specifically in this book, I mentioned, The Herald of Coming Good. That is his hope that it would be possible to found on the earth, Clubs of a new kind. He took this extremely seriously, although he was never able to realize it during his life. He saw that it was necessary for people to be able to meet and to exchange experiences. But the way they do so under present circumstances is foolish because they usually exchange experiences and converse only about things that are trivial and external, or else they do so under highly formal and ritualistic conditions. Gurdjieff wanted to see the possibility for people to meet and share in experience so that many types of people would come in contact with one another, and that understanding of the problem of human life and the way in which people should live should spread. Right up to the end of his life, he used to speak about the gravity of the problem. In other words, what he wanted to do was by no means esoteric, or hidden; on the contrary, he was very much concerned that as many people as possible should realize that there is this problem of human life and that this realization should be shared and faced. He saw that it was inevitable there would be many different ways of interpreting and understanding this, and hoped that some means could be found by which there should be some kind of common ground on the basis of which people could meet. I think he had hoped, during his lifetime, that he would be able to make a definite start towards this, but he was singularly unfortunate. His initial attempt in France, at Fontainebleu, failed and just when he had really prepared things again in the late 1930's, the Second World War broke out. After the war, he was too ill and too near the end of his life to be able to do much, though he did make one very serious effort to found a place outside Paris.

I think that Gurdjieff hoped that what he had discovered and understood about these questions would be freely spread among people, without any sort of secrecy, and that people should be made to realize that it is possible for anyone who is prepared to do so, to participate in the task of living his or her life in such a way that it is productive in the Creative World. For some people, this can be carried very much further and they can attain what Gurdjieff called 'accelerated results.' He certainly believed that it is possible for other people, without having the same intensity of living for themselves, to participate in this general process. It is the obligation of those who have more strength in this field to share with others, so that there can be a general spreading of this understanding of the way of life and the ability to live it. This is intimately connected with the transformation of substances. It means, in simple language, that those who are spiritually strong can help those who are spiritually weak - not by their outward actions alone but by lending them a supply of the "substance of work." It is somewhat analagous to the "Queen Substance" that the Queen Bee produces and that makes possible all the activity of the worker bees. This very important notion was first explained to me by Gurdjieff in July 1923 and I have referred to it briefly in my book, Witness (p. 124). If you can understand this, you will have come near to the very essence of the meaning of man's life on the earth. Gurdjieff had the power to produce the 'substance of work' and those of us who knew him were able to draw upon it. But there are other and more powerful reserves of this substance than any one man can produce.

So we come back again to the question of

where Gurdjieff himself stood in relation to the total work proceeding on the earth. Much confusion has arisen on account of Gurdjieff's own special way of living personally that I referred to earlier as the Way of Blame. People have been led to think that it was necessary that the work should be repellant. I am sure this was not Gurdjieff's intention. All that he wanted to avoid - was that people should become dependent upon him, that they should direct their suggestibility towards him and turn to him as a kind of leader-figure. His aim was that people should become free. It was only for himself, personally, that this particular method was applicable, and when he saw anyone else imitating it, he turned on them with the utmost ferocity and said, 'This is quite unnecessary for you and stupidity that you should do this yourself.' In other words, if people who were connected with him, began to imitate his rather incomprehensible behaviour and attract blame towards themselves he was quite merciless in pointing out that this was quite unnecessary for them and therefore totally wrong. It was only necessary for him because of the peculiar task which he had set himself.

He certainly was under some special kind of obligation, that in the particular work he had to do, he should not assume a position of being a great teacher, with a large number of pupils depending upon him. It was often very obvious that with the greatest of ease, if he had chosen to do so, he could have exercised the power he had to attract people. He could have had thousands of people round him, and he could have spread his methods, which are really extraordinarily valuable for people who wish to live their lives better among thousands of people instead of a relatively small number. But he deliberately abstained from anything of this sort for some reason which I think I know, but which it would not be right to speak about this time.

I have tried to give you some notion about this peculiar man and the way his work developed, and I think that it is much more important in relation to the whole human problem than most people realize, that is to say, Gurdjieff was making a very great effort to play his part, but it is not, by any means, the whole story. There is a whole process going on in the world just now; a whole creative activity concerned with lifting man over the present interval into a new cycle, so that this new cycle should be entered without too serious handicaps from the past. This is happening in so many ways, with such an intricate interworking, that as I grow older and see more and more of it - I happen to live in such a situation that I see it in many parts of the world - I am really in wonderment at the extraordinary power, the super-human intelligence and consciousness that is directing the hidden affairs of mankind at the present time.

Before I finish this talk I would like to say

something to you about what I think it is possible for us to contribute at this moment.

I have not given these lectures because I wanted to arouse new interest in Gurdjieff; but because at the moment things are developing in such a way that I believe that his great aim in connection with people can now be carried a certain step further. I think many of you are aware that in England and other countries, developments are taking place with the aim of making it possible for people who are in search of the Creative Activity to have the opportunity of meeting. I want to invite you, if any of you are interested in pursuing this further, to learn about the fields of creative activity, including that of one's self-study, in which we are engaged. If you are interested, I would like you to get directly in touch with me. If any of you care to write to me and tell me about your interest; then I will let you know about the plans we have for this autumn that aim at carrying this work further and opening up various possibilities that have been rather neglected for some time past. My purpose in giving these lectures was not simply to chat about Gurdjieff; but also to tell you that there are certain directions in which I think it is now possible to carry forward this work in a very productive way.